INISHMURRAY

This tiny island off the coast of Sligo is rich in
history and prehistory. Site of an early Christian settlement
and, more recently, of a hardy group of settlers who sketched out
a living through fishing, poteen and butter-making, the island was
finally evacuated in the 1940s. In this book the history,
archaeology, customs, religious rites and beliefs of
the Inishmurray folk live on.

"Here ... is a wonderful book about Inishmurray, the ruin-rich
island off the Sligo coast ... Buy this book and keep it."
Irish Independent

"a most readable and informative narrative of the
human story of the island."
Irish Wildbird Conservancy

PATRICK HERAUGHTY is an ex-islander who spent the first twelve years of his life on Inishmurray. Later he trained as a doctor and practised in Sligo. An amateur archaeologist he was Vice President of the Royal Society of Antiquaries of Ireland and President of the Sligo Field Club. He is now retired and living in Dublin.

INISHMURRAY

Ancient Monastic Island

THE O'BRIEN PRESS

DUBLIN

This revised edition first published 1982 by The O'Brien Press Ltd.,
20 Victoria Road, Rathgar, Dublin 6, Ireland.
Reprinted in paperback 1996.

British Library Cataloguing-in-Publication Data
A catalogue reference for this book is available from the British Library

ISBN 0-86278-473-5

2 3 4 5 6 7 8 9 10
96 97 98 99 00 01 02 03 04 05

The O'Brien Press receives assistance from
The Arts Council/An Chomhairle Ealaíon

Typesetting, editing, layout, design: The O'Brien Press Ltd.
Cover photographs: Professor Michael Herity
Cover separations: Lithoset Ltd.
Printing: Colour Books Ltd.

CONTENTS

To my own folk of Inishmurray,
all those who have gone beyond
and to those who are still with us.

PREFACE

The production of this revised edition is more of a credit to Martin Timoney, B.A., of Keash, county Sligo, than it is to me. When I told Martin that, because so much more material had come to light since the publication of the original work and that some minor corrections were necessary, I had asked O'Brien Press to publish a new edition, he entered on the project with enthusiasm. He researched material, studied all previous works on and references to Inishmurray, cross-checking and demanding accuracy in detail. He came up with many original ideas and advised on the placing of the new material. All his skills as an expert archaeologist and as a teacher were brought to bear on the production. His wife Mary helped us with her extensive historical and archaeological knowledge. Mary Gormley did much of the original computerisation of the text.

The contribution of that most gentlemanly of scholars Dr Don Cotton, of Sligo Regional Technical College, expert not only in his chosen subjects of Botany, Zoology and Ornithology, but also in the ancillary sciences of Geology and Climatology, is an invaluable addition to the text.

Aideen Ireland of the Royal Irish Academy spared no effort in her diligent, iota precise research on the contribution of Roger Chambers Walker to the acquisition and placement of archeological finds from county Sligo and also on the saga of the *Soiscéal Molaise*.

My thanks to Dr Niamh Whitfield of the British Museum for supplying the drawing of the St. Molaise Bell and to Professor Michael Herity of University College Dublin for permission to use the front and back cover photographs. Dr Stefan Bergh of Stockholm whose doctoral thesis was on the archaeology of Cuil Irra, county Sligo, was more than helpful with his interpretation of R.C. Walker's activities. Siobhán de hÓir of the Royal Society of Antiquaries of Ireland was of invaluable assistance in assessing Vallency with regard to Inishmurray. John McTernan, recently retired county Sligo Librarian, historian and author, researched many difficult phases of recorded history and made available the Wakeman collection of drawings in Sligo County Library. Dr Richard Thorn of Castlebar Regional Technical College checked the geology and probable "genesis" of Inishmurray. Also I am in debt to John O'Hara for his help willingly given and to my nephew Liam Kelly for his help on the population records of Inishmurray.

Finally, I am most grateful to the O'Brien Press for having agreed to publish this edition, for their expertise in its publication and for their unfailing courtesy.

Patrick Heraughty
1996

I have taken an unjustifiable risk in having waited so long to record my memories of Inishmurray. Evening is closing in and soon no one who has lived an adult life on the island will be left. There has, however, been some gain from my procrastination. The placenames of the island have recently been almost exhaustively recorded and explained by Mícheál MacCarthaigh. It was only in 1975 that I learned of James Harte's important discovery of a possible food vessel on the island. I am still learning of traditions from the few islanders left who are my seniors. And I have received valuable comment from archaeologists who have made me aware of many previously unnoticed facts. However, the passing days warn that I should wait no longer. This book is an attempt to record the human story of Inishmurray seen, of necessity, in the prism of such historical facts as are known and the half-light of prehistory.

I wish to thank all those who encouraged me. Some are no longer here: the late Jim Gallagher once the national school teacher at Drumkeerin, county Leitrim, my great friend Michael Cahalane who until his untimely death was secretary of the Sligo Field Club, and my sometime fellow undergraduate Tom Kennedy who did so much to try to preserve the monuments of Inishmurray. Others who still help and bear with me are Des Smyth, Secretary of the Sligo Field Club, and F.P. Kitchen of Ballisodare. I do not know of anyone who could get the same compulsive volume of meaning into the "must" of "you must!" as Pat can when trying to encourage a laggard. Nor can I forget the Reverend Denis Meehan, then Professor of Greek in Maynooth, now living in Los Angeles, who long ago insisted that I should do what I now attempt.

My special informant and mentor was Domnick Harte of Moneygold who with his brother James Harte of Bedford, England, gave me valuable assistance. Mícheál MacCarthaigh has been a great help, and we did enjoy our research into the placenames and tales of long ago. Mrs Eileen Doyle of Churchtown, Dublin, gave me the final push and very generously typed from my all but indecipherable notes, the first legible transcript. My daughter Sheila transcribed from my original tapes, and my niece Ceola Kelly typed the later part of the first transcript also under the handicap of my written notes. Mrs McGowan eventually put it all together, and Mrs Ann O'Donovan very efficiently prepared the final draft.

Late in the day but invaluable in directing research came Aodán O'Higgins of Strandhill, county Sligo. George Gmelch's selective photography is a major contribution to the work. Sharon Gmelch's editing is professionally superb and working with Michael O'Brien and his team at 20 Victoria Road will remain one of my most pleasant memories.

I very gratefully acknowledge the permission, from *An Cumann Logainmneacha*, to reproduce from the May 1971 issue of *Dinnseanchas* compiled by Mícheál Mac-Carthaigh. The Ulster Museum gave me permission to reproduce the Welch photographs. The Royal Society of Antiquaries gave permission to reproduce the photograph of "The Holy Well". The Ordnance Survey granted permission to reproduce the map of Inishmurray. The Public Record Office, London, supplied and gave permission to use the 1589 map of the Sligo coast showing the location of the Armada wreck. The Admiralty gave permission to reproduce their map of Donegal Bay.

Patrick Heraughty

1982

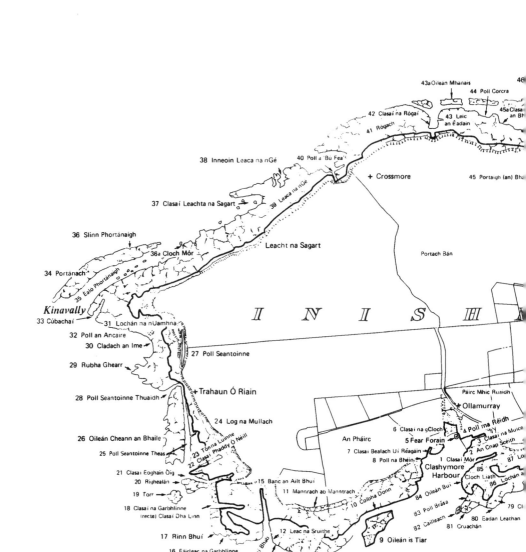

43a Oileán Mhanais

44 Poll Corcra

42 Clasaí na Rógaí

43 Leic an Éadáin

45a Clasa an Bh

41 Rógach

38 Inneoin Leaca na nGé

40 Poll a Bú Fea

+ Crossmore

45 Portaigh (an) Bha

37 Clasaí Leachta na Sagart

39 Leaca na nGé

36 Slinn Phortánaigh

38a Cloch Mór

Leacht na Sagart

Portach Bán

34 Portánach

35 Ealo Phortánaigh

Kinavally

33 Cúbachaí

31 Lochán na nUamhna

II   N   I   I   S   H   I   II

32 Poll an Ancaire

30 Cladach an Ime

27 Poll Seantoinne

29 Rubha Ghearr

+ Trahaun Ó Riain

Páirc Mhic Ruaidh

+ Ollamurray

28 Poll Seantoinne Thuaidh

24 Log na Mullach

6 Clasaí na gCloch

4 Poll na Réidh

26 Oileán Cheann an Bhaile

An Pháirc

5 Fear Forain

3 Clasaí na Muice

2 An Cnap Sceith

25 Poll Seantoinne Theas

7 Clasaí Bealach Uí Réagáin

1 Clasaí Mór

87 Lo

23 Tonna Luinne

8 Poll na Bhéin

Clashymore
Harbour

85

22 Clasaí Phaddy O'Neill

Cloch Liath

86 Lochán

21 Clasaí Eoghain Óig

84 Oileán Buí

79 Cl

20 Righealán

15 Banc an Ailt Bhuí

83 Poll Brása

19 Torr

11 Mannrach ab Manntrach

10 Colba Donn

80 Eadan Leathan

18 Clasaí na Garbhlinne
(recte) Clasaí Dha Linn

82 Cailleach

81 Cruachán

17 Rinn Bhuí

12 Leac na Sruithe

9 Oileán is Tiar

16 Fáirleac na Garbhlinne

14 Clasaí Bhab

13 Poll Bhillí

The placen
Mícheál
Pat

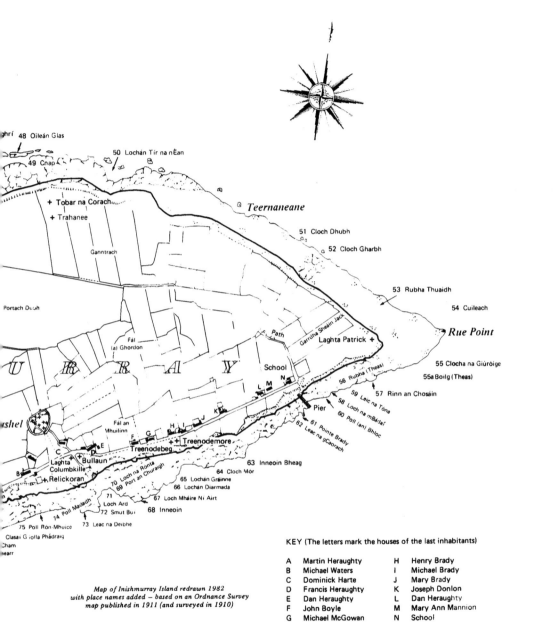

ghrí 48 Oileán Glas

50 Lochán Tír na nÉan

49 Cnap

+ Tobar na Corach

+ Trahanee

Ganntrach

Portach Dubh

Fál (a) Ghordon

U R R A Y

School

Path

Garrúha Sheáin Jack

Laghta Patrick +

Teernaneane

51 Cloch Dhubh

52 Cloch Gharbh

53 Rubha Thuaidh

54 Cuileach

● **Rue Point**

55 Clocha na Giúróige

55a Boilg (Theas)

56 Rubha (Theas)

57 Rinn an Chosáin

59 Laic na Tóna

58 Loch na mBádaí

60 Poll (an) Bhloc

61 Pointe Brady

62 Leac na gCaorach

Pier

Fál an Mhuilinn

Treenodebeg

+ + Treenodemore

C D E
B
Laghta
Columbkille + Bullaun
Relickoran

70 Loch na Ronta
69 Port an Churaigh

71
Loch Ard
72 Smut Buí

68 Inneoin

75 Poll Rón-Mhuice
74 Poll Madadh
73 Leac na Deibhe

Clasaí G íolla Phádraig
Cham
earr

63 Inneoin Bheag

64 Cloch Mór

65 Lochán Gráinne

66 Lochán Diarmada

67 Loch Mháire Ní Airt

*Map of Inishmurray Island redrawn 1982
with place names added – based on an Ordnance Survey
map published in 1911 (and surveyed in 1910)*

0   500   1 000 Feet

lied by
and

KEY (The letters mark the houses of the last inhabitants)

A	Martin Heraughty	H	Henry Brady
B	Michael Waters	I	Michael Brady
C	Dominick Harte	J	Mary Brady
D	Francis Heraughty	K	Joseph Donlon
E	Dan Heraughty	L	Dan Heraughty
F	John Boyle	M	Mary Ann Mannion
G	Michael McGowan	N	School

✚ Christian Monuments, Statues, Churches etc.

Inishmurray, just a few kilometres off the Sligo coast, rises only twenty-one metres above sea level at its highest point on the western end. The island was inhabited from the sixth century and contains the most complete remains of an early Christian settlement in Europe.

CHAPTER 1

Ancient Monastic Island

Inishmurray is a small island off the coast of county Sligo in northwest Ireland. It is situated roughly seven kilometres from the nearest point on the mainland shore. Other islands off Sligo's coast are no more than metres from the mainland, and even those of neighbouring Donegal and Mayo are much nearer to their respective shores. Inhabited for centuries, but now deserted by man, Inishmurray today contains the most complete remains of an early Irish monastic settlement as well as the ruins of its nineteenth century houses. From the available evidence it appears that Inishmurray was continuously inhabited from the sixth century, although the population waxed and waned through the years. And it is not unreasonable to assume that there were people on the island before this, perhaps hundreds of years before, since Inishmurray would have been an ideal location for the Formorian sea marauders who once lived on Ireland's offshore islands. Two locations on the island suggest a prehistoric settlement, but definitive archaeological proof awaits future excavation. At its height in 1880, Inishmurray boasted a population of 102 persons. But this had fallen to forty-six by the time of its evacuation in 1948 when the relative affluence of life on the mainland and in towns and cities, from nearby Sligo to London and Birmingham, drew people away.

Inishmurray is low lying, rising approximately 21 metres (70 feet) above sea level at its highest point on the western end and sloping to sea level on the east. It is only one and half kilometres long (one mile) and less than a kilometre across (a half-mile) at its widest part and resembles a bay leaf in shape, with Rue Point the point of the leaf and Kinavally the foot stalk. Of its 90.25 hectares (223 acres), only 25.50 (63 acres) are good arable land. The rest is shallow peat. Indeed, in some places, it is subsoil from which the peat has been stripped. The rock beneath the soil is sandstone, while the rest of north Sligo (with the exception of sandstone outcrops at Mullaghmore and Rooskeeragh Point and the Bowmore Rocks), like most of Ireland,

Mullaghmore

ATLANTIC OCEAN

INISHMURRAY

CLIFFONY

Streedagh Pt.

MONEYGOLD

Benbulben Mtn.

GRANGE

LISSADELL

Drumcliff Bay

DRUMCLIFF

ROSSES POINT

SLIGO BAY

SLIGO

Lough Gill

0   2   4   6
Scale in miles

is limestone country. But Inishmurray and its submerged rock, lying both east and west of the island, are sandstone. This suggests that the island is the highest remaining point of an arm of land that once extended from Mullaghmore on the mainland to the west of Inishmurray. It became an island around 7,000 B.C. when a notable rise in sea level the world over resulted in the submerging of much coastal land. At the western end of the island long, deep inlets of sea form natural harbours and excellent swimming pools. They are known as "classeys" from the Irish *clais* meaning furrow. Only at Classiebawn at Mullaghmore on the mainland is this word used to describe a sea inlet.

The island is poor in natural resources. The flora is that found in any peaty, coastal soil – sea pinks in profusion, tormentil, bog cotton, buttercups, orchids, bluebells, daisies, heathers, and such. Centaurey blooms profusely in August and was known by the islanders as "the Blessed Virgin flower", probably because of the occurrence of the Feast of the Assumption on 15 August. The primrose does not grow there and there are no trees or shrubs. The blackberry bush is the nearest representative of a shrub and this is scarce – at blackberry time one had to be up at dawn to make a worthwhile collection. There are no lakes on the island, just three small pools in places where turf has been removed.[1]

There are few animals on the island. Not even rats live there, indeed the clay of the island was believed to be fatal to rats. Mainland farmers often got clay from Inishmurray to spread about their farmland to kill rats. The great silence on its effect, however, makes for suspicion of its efficacy. Quite probably no rats ever got to the island because they would scramble out of the small boats before they left the mainland. There are mice, but these did not arrive until someone had stabbed a neighbour's horse and in retribution the drops of blood turned into mice, or so the islanders said. The most unusual animal is a small lizard known as a "mankeeper" which reputedly jumps into the mouth of anyone who stoops to drink water out of a well. Seals are found on the island's rocky shores and a variety of birds visit its barren surface. My grandfather had a pet seal for many years. He made a shelter for it in a small rock cave near the high water mark. It was an excellent weather forecaster as it always left and went out into deep waters twenty-four hours or more before a storm arose. Today Inishmurray is a bird sanctuary, but there has been a marked change in the bird population since the islanders left.

Birds such as the sparrow that once frequented the island have almost disappeared. The lapwing, once the most common bird, is now a rarity. Rock pippits are now also very few. Crows and blackbirds are not found on the island, although migrant thrushes do come seasonally, as do swallows, swifts, and corncrakes in large numbers. The preponderance today consists of sea birds, with a marked increase in gulls. Shell ducks and eider ducks have become common since the islanders left, and Inishmurray is now the southern-most station of the eider duck.

Classeymore, the island's natural harbour

Access to Inishmurray was always unpredictable. There was no enclosed harbour and all boats had to be taken out of the water and stowed safely on the rocks out of the sea's reach. As a result, the islanders used small boats of eight metres (28 feet) or less. In winter, contact with the mainland might be severed for up to six weeks. Even in summer, a week's isolation was not unusual. The one road on the island was built in the later part of the nineteenth century. It runs from the eastern to the western entrances of the peaty common which covers most of the island surface. The twelve remaining houses stand on the northern part of this road and face due south. The roofs were originally of thatch but subsequent rooms added to the original structures were slate-roofed. Due to the wet conditions and the use of straw as the thatching material, the roofs were freshly thatched about every third year.

During the last century and until the island's evacuation, the main economic activity on Inishmurray was the making of illegal whiskey which was sold to retailers on the mainland. Fishing, especially for fish that could be cured and later sold to the mainland, ranked next. Getting freshly caught fish to market on time was always a problem. Edible seaweed like *crannach* (often miscalled "dilisk" in the shops) and carrigeen moss, known on Inishmurray as "*fúdar*", were collected, dried and sold in Sligo town. Farming was at subsistence level, with the potential cash bonus of one to four young cattle for sale each year. The families on two holdings were also able to produce enough homemade butter and surplus eggs to sell to mainland shops.

Though isolated and poor, Inishmurray was a rich and satisfying environment in which to live. It was a close community in which people were friendly and helpful. Though young people might tease or make fun of older persons, they were always kind. And no one was allowed to be in want – a helping hand always reached out. When someone was old or ill, for example, a group of younger people would gather, without being asked, to save their hay, cut their turf, plant their potatoes, or offer to transport their cattle to the mainland. Young and old alike gathered together for festive occasions and to play games or listen to Crimley, the island wit, tell saga tales and stories of long ago. At a dance the older people would sit around to comment on and encourage the young. Fellowship and community spirit were strong. Indeed, islanders often felt "lonely" on trips to the mainland and longed to return home.

In this book I hope not only to document the important early monastic history of Inishmurray but also to provide a record of its people, their traditions, and the conditions they lived under while it is still within living memory. As one of the few islanders remaining who lived to adulthood on Inishmurray, I feel an obligation to write what I can while there are still others who can help and correct me. I have used archival material and published archaeological and historical accounts, but there is still much historical and professional archaeological research to be done.

The cashel appears to the right, with its surrounding wall, *Teampall na mBan* (the "church of the women") to the left.

Prehistoric Site and Monastic Remains

As yet the prehistory of Inishmurray is practically untouched. In 1938 James Harte, a native of Inishmurray, found a collapsed cist burial near the inlet known as Classeymore. It contained what, from his description, was an ornamented food vessel of a type associated with burials dating from the second millennium B.C. A brief survey of the area by Professor Estyn Evans of Queen's University, Belfast, also led him to suggest there was evidence of human occupation at the site in prehistoric times. Other archaeologists have subsequently agreed. Martin Timoney, for one, concurs and observed that one of the side slabs of a "sailor's grave" nearby is *in situ*, that is, in its original position, indicating an earlier burial at the site. The grave appears today as a depression of rectangular outline with a large flat stone set firmly in the ground on its edge. The stone is about 1.6 metres (4 feet 6 inches) long and the portion of the stone above ground is almost 0.91 metres (3 feet) high. It appears to be part of the sidewall of a prehistoric stone tomb chamber. Without excavation dating is not possible but such a chamber would date earlier than 1800 B.C. Such evidence of prehistoric occupation is tantalising, but definitive proof awaits a detailed archaeological investigation. The Sites and Monuments Record suggests that there was a promontory fort at the southwest corner of the island but I think it is more a reflection of the end of the farmable land in this area.

The first historical information about Inishmurray is a reference, contained in the *Martyrology of Donegal*, to a monastic settlement there. The reference reads as follows: "August 12 Molaise. Laisrén, son of Delgán of Inis Muiredaich. He it was, who, at the Cross of Ath-Imlaise, pronounced sentence on St. Columba." The sentence pronounced was one of banishment from Ireland becuse of St. Columba's (Colmcille) responsibility for the battle of Cúl Dreimhne in north Sligo. The battle took place in either 555 or 561 A.D.[1] Thus it would appear that the monastic settlement was founded some years earlier, circa 520 A.D. The settlement on Inishmurray is said to have come from Aughris in Tireragh, county Sligo, itself a cell or offshoot of the monastery at Skreen, a foundation of Colmcille. There is a strong oral tradition and some impressive evidence of an association between the Inishmurray settlement and St. Colmcille. The Inishmurray foundation was established by St. Molaise who seems also to have been referred to as Muirdeach (and also Laisrén) in some early documents. The name Muirdeach is retained in the Irish name of the island, *Inis Muirdeach*. Further successive abbots on Inishmurray appear to have continued to use the name Molaise, a name which may have been compounded from "*mo laogh se*" (*mo* meaning my, *laogh* meaning calf but also "dear" and "pet", and the emphatic suffix *se*).

Later references found in the *Annals of Ireland* (The Four Masters) help us visualise some of the events, mainly deaths, taking place in these early years. In 747 A.D. "Dicolle, son of Meinide abbot of Inishmurray died." In 798 A.D. "Mac Laisre, the learned, of Inishmurray, died." In 807 A.D., "Inishmurray was burned by the foreigners, and they attacked Roscomain [Roscommon]." This reference is to the Viking attacks then taking place around Ireland's coast. And finally, in 1612 A.D. "Moyleen O'Dalaigh died on All Souls Day and was buried on Inismurray after bearing triumph from the world and the devil." It is not clear if the monastery still existed in 1612 when this last reference to a burial (that of Moyleen O'Dalaigh) is made. Oral tradition indicates that the monks had left the island at the end of the twelfth century when the O'Connors ousted the O'Dowds as masters of the nearby mainland. However, it is quite clear from Cuellar's account of his escape from the wrecked *Sancta Maria* of the Spanish Armada in 1588, that a monastery still existed at *Stáid* – the mainland "stopping house" of the Inishmurray monks. This could mean that there was still a monastery on Inishmurray but it could also mean that some other monks had taken over the *Stáid* house. Our understanding of this period is hampered by a number of factors. Accidental fires and those caused by enemy action destroyed much written material in Irish monastic houses. Moreover, Irish religious communities are accepted as having been some of the world's worst record keepers. To the best of available knowledge the monastic settlement on Inishmurray was founded circa 520 A.D. and ended in the latter part of the twelfth century, although Cuellar's evidence and the reference to Moyleen O'Dalaigh's burial suggest that it might have continued into the early seventeenth century.[2]

The monastic life on Inishmurray would have been the same as that of other Irish monastic communities or, as it came to be known, the "Columban" monastic life. The monks lived in communities run by a superior often known as an abbot. The abbacy was often hereditary in that it remained in the family of the founder. The abbot had a parallel lay superior know as a "*Coarb*" and sometimes as an "*Eireannach*". The

The *clochann* Tory Bhrennell with, on the left, the gable of *Teach na Teine*, part of *Teach Molaise,*
in the middle distance, some ruined houses and, across on the mainland, the Dartry range,

original distinction was that the *Coarb* was celibate and the *Eireannach* was not necessarily so, but the distinction later lapsed. Much of the monks' time would have been spent in private prayer and adoration apart from the following of the prescribed rule of celebrating Mass and saying the Office at the appointed times. They also engaged in farming and other manual work. Moreover, they achieved a high degree of stone carving skill as evidenced by the profusion of beautifully ornamented cross-inscribed slabs and rounded stones they left behind.

The "stations", a devotion which involved walking prescribed circuits about stone altars while praying, were a frequent feature of Irish monastic life, especially, it would appear, on islands with religious community associations. They may originally have been a pagan custom which became Christianised, like many other such customs. The pagan priests of *Crom Cruach*, for example, were said to have "daily in their mystic ring turned the maledictive stones". The turning of the maledictive stones was a possible variation of the Inishmurray station. The monks would have constructed the stations and almost certainly performed the associated devotional exercises at them. There was a similar station, the *Turas Mor*, on Tory Island off the north Donegal coast and there is a similar smaller round on the island of St. Patrick's Purgatory in Lough Derg, Donegal. In many other parts of Ireland "rounds" are done but generally at only a single isolated station.

THE RUINS

The monastic remains standing on Inishmurray today lie principally within the enclosure known as the "cashel" and were restored by the then Board of Works (now the Office of Public Works) at the end of the last century. But there are other remains, associated with the monastic settlement, outside the cashel and dotted around the periphery of the island, notably *Teampall na mBan* and its associated enclosure and the stations. The cashel wall was most likely built in the ninth century, when the Viking raids began, as a defensive wall around the pre-existing structures.

I have no set idea of the date of the cashel wall. It may well have pre-dated the monastic elements within it. On the other hand, tradition is that up to the time of St. Colmcille there was none other than monks living on the island. They would have heard of the Norse raid on Lambay and would have had time to defend themselves by building the cashel wall, perhaps even adding a wooden palisade, imported from the mainland, for further defense.

The earliest plan of the cashel that I am aware of is that published by Charles Vallency (1786, Pl. V – Fig. 1). As we do not have any evidence that Vallency was ever on Inishmurray it is most likely that the plan was that made by Beranger in 1779 (Wilde 1870, 132). The plan in Grose (1791) is a defective copy of that in Vallency.

The monument illustrated by Vallency (1786, Pl. V – Fig. 2) is *Roilig Ódhráin*, the only one to have a rectangular enclosure and a long pillarstone. Vallency derived the name Inishmurray from *Muidhr* or sun stone, equating the pillar on *Roilig Ódhráin* with the sun stone. Ledwich, as editor of Grose, was not having any of this and neither should we. Significantly Ledwich omitted the sun-stone monument of Mahoody on Elephanta in the East Indies from his copy of Vallency's plate V.

The original height of the cashel wall is no longer ascertainable, but on the northern side it is still more than 4.57 metres (15 feet) high. Its width varies from 2.44 to 3.05 metres (8 -10 feet). It contains several wall-chambers, like those at *Staigue Fort* in county Kerry, the *Grianán* of *Aileach* in county Donegal and *Cashel Óir* and *Clogher* in county Sligo. Its defensive stepping is also well preserved on the western and northern sides. Local tradition claims that sometime during the eighteenth century the cashel wall was used for target practice by Royal Navy gunboats, and that, while they easily reached the nearer southern wall, they failed to get the range of the northern wall. I was told by a man who worked on the restoration that "oakum" cannon balls were found in the collapse of the southern wall. Cockle shells in large quantities and some deer skulls were also found. Since there are no beaches on Inishmurray, the cockles must have been imported to vary the diet. And as it is very unlikely that deer roamed on such a small island, their carcases must also have been imported. To the right of the gateway, which was fashioned by the Board of Works restorers, is a mound said to contain spoil from the wall collapse. This mound requires detailed archaeological investigation. The cashel wall has three low, ground-level openings or open entrances, with defensive chambers, in the eastern and northern sections. They were probably the original entrances to the cashel; both *doras an uisce* ("the water door") and the doorway fashioned by the Board of Works restorers are later additions.[3]

The cashel wall encloses one-fourteenth of a hectare (0.33 acre) which is divided into three parts by low partition walls. The enclosed area contains a number of buildings including: *Teampall na bhFear* ("church of the men"), *Teampall na Teine* or *Teach na Teine* ("church or house of the fire") *Teach Molaise* ("Molaise's house"), *Tory Bhrennell* (*Tórradh Bhruinnille*, meaning "wake of the virgin"), and *Tráthán an Charghais* ("the Lenten retreat"). *Teampall na bhFear*, also known as *Teampall Molaise* and *Teampall Mór*, appears to have been the principal church of the monastery. *Teampall na Teine* was probably the monastery's kitchen and would have been the only building in which a fire was permitted. It does in fact contain a square central hearth. Oral tradition on the island claimed that if all the fires on the island were accidentally or intentionally extinguished, a sod of turf placed on the hearth would ignite spontaneously. In the last century, this hearth was said to have been desecrated by an "unbeliever", but it revenged itself by igniting and consuming the desecrator. Islanders pointed to some human bones in an alcove in the wall of the church as proof of this incident.

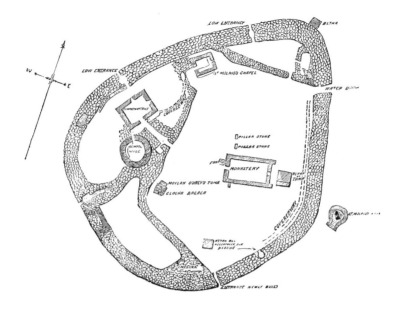

Above: ground plan of the cashel as drawn by Wakeman and, below, a more recent aerial shot of the cashel and enclosed structures with field walls and lane leading to the cashel. The walls were probably built in the ninth century as a defence against Viking raiders.

Teach Molaise was believed to have been St. Molaise's house. A high stone altar on the eastern wall is called *Áltóir Molaise* ("Molaise's Altar"), and a low, stone bench on the southern wall is called *Leaba Molaise* or "Molaise's bed".

At the junction of the two altars stood the Statue of St. Molaise. After the island was abandoned it was moved for safety to the National Museum of Ireland in 1949. The most modern research on the 1.27 metre (4.7 feet) high statue is that done by Fergus O'Farrell in conjunction with his reproduction of copies of it for the public park in Grange and the Cathedral of the Immaculate Conception in Sligo. His article was published in 1987. His opinion is that "it would therefore seem rather unlikely that it dates from a time much subsequent to the twelfth century" (1987, 208). While the arms are gone it is clear that the right hand was raised in blessing. The left hand probably held a crozier. He points out that the head was originally one piece with the body and that the hollowing of the back of the statue was a means of preventing surface cracking of the timber. Since then O'Farrell has made a 21 cm (8.27 inches) high replica of the statue from a 3,500 year old piece of bog yew. This was presented to me by Sligo County Council on 16 February 1994 in recognition of many years service on The National Monuments Advisory Committee of Sligo County Council.

Loftus Jones of Ballisodare attempted to burn the statue of St. Molaise and failed. He then cut off the arms and threw all into the sea; only the statue was subsequently recovered. Tradition has it that on the return voyage from the island Jones became deranged, evident in the fact that he attempted to bite off his own shoulders.

There has been considerable chipping away of the front of the base of the statue. This was not done by a desecrator but by the islanders themselves in the early years of this century and perhaps the latter years of the last century. Islanders who had relatives abroad, generally in the USA, chipped off small pieces from that part of the statue and sent them as relics to such relatives who at the time might be in trouble, generally due to illness. In the tens of this century, Fr. Brian O'Crehan, curate at Grange, arranged to have the practice stopped. On one of his visits to the island he gathered the people to the cashel and having blessed a number of religious medals he touched each medal to the statue of St. Molaise before distributing them to the various householders. He asked that, if relics were requested by relatives, medals be sent instead. This worthy preservation effort was immediately and totally successful.

Tory Bhrennell is a large beehive building made entirely of stone, including its corbelled roof. A long stone bench runs along the northern part of the wall. It resembles a school bench, and gave rise to the occasionally-used name – "the school house". One authority, familiar with similar buildings in Greece, has suggested that it was a charnel-house. This is supported by a local story explaining the meaning of the name *Tory Bhrennell* (or more correctly, *Tórradh Bhruinnille*), the "wake" or "waking place of the virgin". Peggy Harte, an old woman at the time she explained the name to me, noted: "She must have been very well thought of when she was

Above: Slab-covered passageway joining the south wall of the cashel to *Teach na Teine*, the "house of fire", which was believed to have been the monastic kitchen.

Below: *Teach an Allais* or the "sweat-house", the Irish equivalent of the Turkish bath. The nearby well may well have been the cold bath that completed the "steaming" process.

allowed to be waked there." She was referring to the fact that only men were buried in the cashel because it was a cloister, while women were buried in *Teampall na mBan*. The *Tráthán an Charghais* ("Lenten retreat") is another beehive structure but this time partly incorporated into the wall of the cashel. It is partitioned in two, and the smaller room has an "upstairs" section. Some recent writings on Inishmurray have referred to this as a sweat-house, but it is not. The construction of sweat-houses followed an established plan and the small, two-storey chamber incorporated in the west wall of this building would be highly atypical. The real sweat-house, *Teach an Allais* ("sweat-house"), stands just outside the cashel wall. It is near *Tobar Molaise*, a deep, covered well located just to the left as one leaves the cashel. Significantly, the well is reached by five descending sandstone steps. Beehive-shaped, stone sweat-houses were the Irish equivalent of the "Turkish bath" or sauna and the nearby well may have been the cold bath which completed the procedure. The water of *Tobar Molaise* was not used for domestic purposes, at least not in modern times. Instead, drinking water was obtained from wells in the rocks beneath the cliffs. There is a third beehive structure near *Tory Bhrennell*, and an underground chamber to the west of this.

In addition to the main buildings in the cashel described above, it also contains a souterrain or underground passage running from the north of *Teach Molaise* towards *Teampall na Teine*. There is a second souterrain inside *Teampall na bhFear*. On the south wall of *Teampall na Teine* is a long chamber covered by slabs that reach the wall plate of the building. There is no entrance to this chamber except between the roof slabs. This gave rise to the colloquial name "jail", into which, it was alleged, unproficient scholars from the nearby "school house" were placed. This may be a construction of the nineteenth century restorers. It is noticeable that within the cashel there are three sub-divisions, three souterrains, three rectangular churches, three beehive structures, three stations and three pillar stones. This strongly suggests a symbolic association with the concept of the Trinity.

THE STATIONS AND INSCRIBED STONES

The inscribed stones and other structures marking Inishmurray's sixteen stations lie around the periphery of the island, beginning just west of *Teampall na mBan* (Church of the women). Directly south of the cashel is the small landing-place of *Port a 'Churry* ("Port of curraghs"). There were no curraghs on the Sligo coast and none between Killala, county Mayo, and Teeling, county Donegal, in living memory. Portcurry Point is the name of the tip of the sandspit south of Strandhill.

The first station, *Leachta Cholmcille* ("memorial altar of Colmcille") is nearby. The stations were followed in a clockwise direction around the island. The second station is about 21.34 metres (70 yards) to the west and is called *Roilig Ódhráin*

Teampall na mBan or the "church of the women" stands a little to the south of the cashel. The name has prompted the belief that a convent once stood here, but no signs of such a building remain.

("Oran's Cemetery"). This was used as a burial place for unbaptised children. It is very likely that when the monastery was in existence, *Roilig Odhráin* was the ordinary burial place on the island; subsequently, men were buried in the cashel and women at *Teampall na mBan*. Here is remarkable evidence of Inishmurray's association with St. Colmcille: at Iona off the west coast of Scotland, where Colmcille established a monastery *circa* 561 A.D., the landing stage is also known as *Port a 'Churry* and the cemetery was also called *Roilig Ódhráin*. According to the island's oral tradition the monks – at the time when the monks were the only inhabitants – requested that they be permitted to keep a cow. But in those early days it was not acceptable for a man to milk a cow, and St. Colmcille used this social taboo as the reason to deny the request. The unchivalrous answer was *"An áit in a mbíonn bó, bíonn bean, agus an áit in a mbíonn bean bíonn miortún"* ("Where there is a cow there is a woman and where there is a woman there is mischief"). The other occasion on which St. Colmcille is said to have visited the island was after the Battle of the Books, when he came to "confess" to Molaise. It was said that when he arrived at *Stáid*, near Streedagh on the mainland, the point from which he proposed to cross to Inishmurray, no boat was available so he spread his cloak on the waters and a path to the island opened before him.[4]

The next station is located near Classymore – the usual landing place on the island. Its name is *Ulla Mhuire* meaning "Mary's altar". The stations were marked by square stone altars with upright cross-inscribed stone slabs in the centre. Two of the altars, *Roilig Ódhráin* and *Clocha Breaca*, have two upright cross-inscribed stones, while another two, *Leachta Cholmcille* and *Leachta Phádraig*, are memorial stone altars. The next station lies at the most western point of the island. It is marked by a small *trahan* or hermit cell called *Trahan Ó Riain* ("O Ryan's Cell"). It appears that some monks, either as a penance or perhaps because of anti-social attitude, left the monastery, at least temporarily, and lived in such *trahans*. It is well known that in orthodox monastery areas, such as Mount Athos in Greece, monks who were associated with the monastery but who were not directly under its rule, lived in similar stone-built cells in the vicinity of the monastery. The rather fanciful name given to this station by John O'Donovan, who carried out the Ordnance Survey in 1836, was unknown on Inishmurray in modern times by even the oldest inhabitants.[5] Just north of *Trahan Ó Riain* a long chasm known as *Poll a (n) Sean Toinne* ("hole of the strong wave") runs inland. Near the floor of this chasm is a mineral spa, and rock doves nest in its cliff wall.

The next station, *Cros Mhór* or "Great Cross", lies to the east. Yet there is no evidence of a cross today, apart from a tiny one inscribed on the altar upright. Not far away is the interesting complex of a *trahan*, *Trahan Aodh* ("Hugh's cell"), located on the heights, and beneath it, *Tobar na Córach* or the "well of the fair [weather]". Together they form the next station. Island tradition states that if a dire emergency arose and storm-tossed seas prevented the launching of a boat, calm would immediately ensue once the prescribed prayers were said and water from the well was poured into the sea.

Clocha Breaca in 1901 with its famous "cursing stones", all of which were cross-inscribed, and two upright cross-inscribed slabs. Several of the plain round stones have been added in recent years.

The next station is *Leachta Phádraig* – the memorial altar to St. Patrick. But it is difficult to identify today. There are several mounds of stones in the immediate vicinity once used by the islanders to dry sea wrack in the summer. The station is located right on the cliff edge. Turning to the west, one comes to the well-preserved stations of the Trinity – *Trionoid Mhór* ("Big Station of the Trinity") and *Trionoid Bheag* ("Small Station of the Trinity'). These are located just in front of the central houses of the island. Directly south of the cashel is the last monument on Inishmurray *Teampall na mBan* or the "church of the women". The name has given rise to the belief that a convent of nuns once existed on the island. No building remains here today except the church whose south wall, once in imminent danger of collapse, has now been very well restored. The name probably arose from the church's use, after lay people had come to live on the island and while the cashel was still a cloister, as a public church where women as well as men could worship.

The circuit of stations just described made up what was known as the "Big Station", traditionally performed on 15 August – the Feast of the Assumption. On this day people from the neighbouring mainland, particularly Cloonagh, joined the islanders in "doing the Big Station".[6] The station was also performed by the islanders at other times of the year, either in supplication for a favour or in thanksgiving for favours received. In dire circumstances, such as in danger of drowning, an individual might promise to perform the station if saved. Performance of the Big Station included observing a number of customs and rituals. As at many other Irish pilgrimage sites, the pilgrim had to fast from the previous midnight and walk the station and rounds barefoot while reciting a set pattern of prayers: at *Teach Molaise* five "Our Fathers", five "Hail Marys", and "The Creed". He or she then climbed to the top of the wall, which is feasible at this point, and made three circuits of the top repeating the same prayers. Since the stones on the wall top are rather sharp and mornings were often damp or dewy, the circuit was none too comfortable, especially for those who were tenderfooted or overweight. When this circuit was completed, the pilgrim knelt again and repeated the prayers. The pilgrim then left the cashel and proceeded from station to station in a clockwise direction, performing two circuits or "rounds" at each station, one outside the retaining wall and one inside the wall around the altar itself. In each case, the pilgrim knelt to say the prayers, then repeated the prayers while walking the circuit, and finally knelt again at the end of the circuit and repeated the prayers a final time. The only variation in this ritual was at *Ulla Mhuire*, *Teampall na mBan* and at *Áltóir Bheag*, just inside the cashel, where five "Hail Marys" not "Our Fathers" were said.

At *Teampall na mBan* rounds were made around the outer wall and around the church. When finished, the pilgrim re-entered the cashel, made a circuit of *Áltóir Bheag* and an altar (whose name had already been lost in 1836) to the east of *Teampall na bhFear*, next was *Teampall na bhFear*, the *Clocha Breaca*, and finally *Teach Molaise*. *Clocha Breaca* was a special station and, as mentioned earlier, has two cross-inscribed uprights and approximately fifty cross-inscribed round stones, the best of which have now been removed from the island for safe-keeping. But two peculiar stones remain. They are hollowed at their broad ends, and have smaller stones that fit into the hollows like corks into a bottle. Their function or purpose has not yet been explained. *Clocha Breaca* translates as "cursing stones", but the islanders used to be sensitive about this and insisted on translating the name as the "speckled stones", pointing out that the stones were cross-inscribed and could hardly have been cursing stones. However, as cursing comes very near to praying "against" someone, it appears that there is justification for the first meaning. When an islander wished to bring down vengeance on an enemy, he or she could perform the Big Station in reverse, walking against the sun, instead of *deiseal* or clockwise, and turning over each of the round stones on *Clocha Breaca* while completing the circuit (typically three rounds of the altar) of that station.[7] A special nine-day preparation for this maledictive station was undertaken. On the first three days an absolute fast was observed, on the second three days only one meal a day was eaten, but on the last three days, normal meals were eaten. Here again the procedure is the reverse of what one would expect. This had decidedly pagan connotations. Similar practices are a feature of many Irish myths and folktales. When the priests of *Crom Cruach* became incensed at Cormac MacAirt's adoption of Christianity, for example, they are said to have "loosed their wrath against the King. Cursed him in his flesh and bones daily in their mystic ring turned the maledictive stones." To perform the Big Station for maledictive purposes was risky for, if you were wrong, the curse was believed to be on your own head.

The Big Station was completed by re-entering *Teach Molaise* and repeating the five "Our Fathers", five "Hail Mary's", and "The Creed". Even at a moderate pace, the station took from three and a half to four hours to complete. Perhaps not suprisingly, there was also a "Wee Station". Full details of this are now difficult to obtain, but it began at *Teach Molaise.* Then the pilgrim went out through one of the low open entrances in the northeastern part of the wall, made a circuit of a station north of the cashel (name unknown), then one of *Ulla Mhuire* at Classeymore, and finally returned to the cashel and finished at *Áltóir Bheag.* A third form of station was that of *Tobar na Córach* ("well of succour from storm"). This involved making a circuit of the altar at *Tobar na Córach* on three consecutive evenings.

Peter Harbison, in a section on Inishmurray in his *Pilgrimage in Ireland, The Monuments and the People* (pp 99-105), correctly expresses surprise that a pilgrimage whose format is so well authenticated and which was performed up to 1948, is nowhere historically recorded.

From the time of Colmcille's last visit to the island in approximately 555 or 561 A.D., until the monks left in the early twelfth century, very little is known of what happened on Inishmurray. How the monks spent their time, apart from the time spent in prayers, can be partially surmised from archaeological finds on the island – the

Or do Muirdeach; hu chomacain; hic dormit – inscribed gravestone originally from the monastic graveyard and later placed in *Teach Molaise*.

inscribed tomb slabs and multitude of beautifully cross-inscribed stones. These are no doubt but a small proportion of the total number produced by the monks. Of the five inscribed slabs, the three smaller ones have been removed from the island in recent years to ensure their safe-keeping. Their small, easily portable size put them at risk had they remained unattended on the island. All three are made of sandstone, although the sandstone of one is not of local origin and may indeed have been an import.

The first inscribed stone carries the inscription "*Or do Murcad*" meaning "Pray for Murcad". The second has a longer, three-line inscription: "*Or do Muirdeach/Hu chomacain/hic dormit*" which means "Pray for Muirdeach scion of Comacan who lies here". This addition of the Latin *hic dormit* to a vernacular inscription is said to be unique in Western Europe. The third inscribed slab is the most interesting but, up to recently, was held to be indecipherable. Indeed a local ballad states that it "was taken to America to be translated there" without success. Recently, with the aid of infra-red photography, it was compared with similar inscribed slabs in Wales and northeastern England and a reasonable, although still tentative, decipherment was made. The stone is coarse-grained and the script is poor and irregular in orientation – the latter letters in some words are smaller than the letters at the beginning of the word and others must be guessed at. Allowing for this, the legend would be: "*Orait ar Nearach do Righne/Crux Talt pro animis nostribus*" or "Pray for Nerach who made [this] Cross of [for?] Talt, on behalf of our souls". The fourth inscribed stone is a large flat tombstone with the inscription "*Or do Con Muirsc*" or "Pray for Con Muirsc". The fifth stone recently re-discovered by a French visitor,

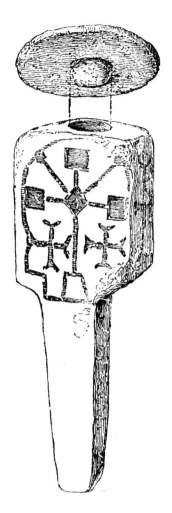

Left: drawing by Wakeman of one of the hollowed-out stones showing stopper that fits into the broad end like a cork in a bottle. Their function is unknown. Right: the west gable of *Teampall Molaise* with pillar stones, at the foot of the stone on the right is a holy water font (saddle quern). In the foreground are *Clocha Breaca*.

Therese Bonnet, lies in the grounds of *Teampall na mBan*. It is a large stone, rectangular in cross-section. It has been suggested that the names on this stone are those of persons who perished in a catastrophe such as a Viking raid and that some names are missing because the stone has been broken. The inscription at present reads " ... *ailad ocus ar Maelbr .../ororc ocus ar Eileise.*" The first word "*ailad*" is probably the latter part of a proper name, and "*Maelbr*" may be the first part of *Maelbrigid*. "*Ocus*" is the modern *agus* ("and"). "*Oroc*" is O'Rorke. Two additional stones with the word "*Crux*" and a third with "*Crux Rete*" were known to W.F. Wakeman when he visited the island in the early 1800s, but are now missing.[9]

The Office of Public Works (OPW) has been working quietly and effectively over the past twenty years on preserving the monuments. Most of the decorated stones have been taken indoors to protect them from futher weather damage. The advice of a team of specialists in the chemistry of stone is being acted on. To facilitate the OPW workers, who spend long periods on the island, a solar panel to provide power has been installed in an extension to the 1899 school and is functioning efficiently. One of the "*Crux*" stones has been recovered and is set into the cashel wall near *Teach Molaise*. The perfection of some of the intricate cross-carvings, particularly on the round stones of the *Clocha Breaca*, is complete, as are the cross-carvings on the uprights of the stations.

Inscribed stones found on the island, which date from the days of the monastic settlement (*c.* 522-1170).

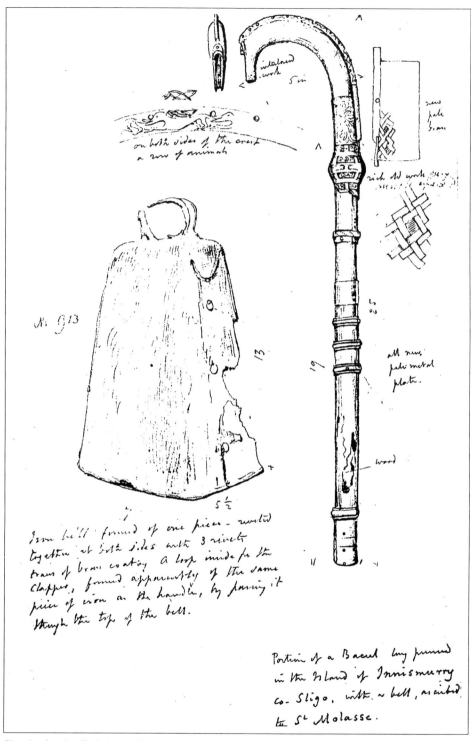

Sketch of early Christian bell and crozier from Inishmurray, now in the collection of the Duke of
Northumberland, who acquired it from Roger Chambers Walker of Sligo.

Archaeological Material from the Monastic Settlement

In recent years much has come to light on material, now housed elsewhere, from the monastic settlement.

I had lost faith in the existence of St. Molaise's Bell. It was not talked about on Inishmurray but was occasionally mentioned in the Grange and Cliffoney areas on the opposite mainland. In fact, bells were sometimes taken to clergy in Sligo and elsewhere with the assurance that they were the authentic St. Molaise's Bell. They all turned out to be trinkets, often given by pedlars, in exchange for some materials collected from householders.

The breakthrough came in 1981 when Dr. Cormac Bourke published a summary of his M.A. thesis under the title "Early Irish Hand Bells", *Journal of the Royal Society of Antiquaries of Ireland*, Vol. 110 (1980), 52-66. In it he listed the Inishmurray Bell which he had located in Alnwick Castle in Northumberland. Roger Chambers Walker of Rathcarrick, county Sligo, sold many of his finds and purchases from Carrowmore and elsewhere through Edward Clibborn and Albert Way in 1851, three years before he died on 7 September 1854 at the young age of forty-eight, apparently of a heart attack. Way acquired the collection for the Duke of Northumberland for whom he was agent with respect to antiquities. When Ian Fisher, archaeologist with the Royal Commission on Ancient and Historical Monuments of Scotland, whose remit included Iona, visited Sligo in 1984 we succeeded in getting to Inishmurray on the second attempt. I told him of Bourke having located the bell. He said straight away that he would go down to Alnwick from Edinburgh the following week to see it. I had a letter from him within a week to say, that not only had he seen the bell, but that St. Molaise's Crozier was also there. A bell and a crozier are normally inseparable attributes of early ecclesiastical rank.

Cormac Bourke has since published a detailed description with illustrations of the crozier and a description and drawings of the bell under the title "A Crozier and bell from Inishmurray and their place in Ninth-Century Irish Archaeology", in *Proceedings of the Royal Irish Academy*, Vol. 85C5 (1985), 145-168 & pl. I-VII. Even for those who are not interested in Inishmurray *per se*, it is well worth acquiring this publication and, naturally so, for those who are interested in the history of the island or of St. Molaise. It is now accepted that both the crozier and the bell were acquired by Roger Chambers Walker by October 1843 at the latest (Bourke 1985, 146), at which time Lord Adare was in *temporary* possession of the *Soiscéal Molaise* (Bourke 1985, 146). We know from the detailed account book kept by Walker from 1836 to 1845 that he visited Inishmurray in August 1837. However, we do not know the route by which the crozier and bell reached Alnwick Castle.

The crozier is listed on p. 183 of the privately published catalogue by J. Collingwood-Bruce *A Descriptive Catalogue of Antiquities, Chiefly British*, at Alnwick Castle, Newcastle-upon-Tyne, 1880 at No. 886 as follows:

> "A portion of a bacul or pastoral staff long preserved in the island of Inishmurray, Co. Sligo, along with a bell (No. 913) ascribed to St. Molaise. The staff is of wood cased with pale metal. The upper portion of it exhibits some rich engraved work. The staff bears the marks of somewhat careless reparation. Length twenty-five inches."

The crozier is 63 cm (25 inches) long and would originally have been over double that length. What has come down to us consists of sixteen metal components (excluding nails) mounted on a wooden core. Its several periods of manufacture and repair are reflected in the multitudinous styles of artwork, a frieze of dog-like creatures running towards the drop of the crozier, traces of interlace or animal ornament on the surface of the crook and quadrangular, basketry, vegetal and floral ornament, also on it. There is evidence for a now-lost secondary crest. The dating ranges from the late ninth century at the earliest to repairs of late medieval, fifteenth, sixteenth and seventeenth centuries.

The catalogue entry for the bell on p. 188 begin: "No. 913. An iron bell preserved with the pastoral staff No. 885 (*recte* 886) and also ascribed to St Molasse." The saint referred to is, of course, St. Molaise. The 32 cm (12.5 inch) high bell is of sheet iron and dates to the eighth or ninth century.

At no point does the Collingwood-Bruce *Catalogue* ascribe either the bell or the crozier to Walker though he does ascribe it to Inishmurray. A letter from Petrie to Adare (Bourke 1985, 146) is the only evidence for Walker being in possession of the bell and crozier. We know from the detailed account book kept by Walker from 1836 to 1845 that he paid £2.00 to Underwood for the old bell on 26 January 1842. Most likely the bell and crozier were acquired together by Walker from a local person and so the bell referred to in the account book as being obtained from Underwood is

St. Molaise's statue (not later than twelfth century), now in the National Museum of Ireland, is unique because of its age: most surviving wooden statues are fourteenth or fifteenth century. The 1.27 metre high figure would probably have had a crozier in the left hand, with the right hand raised in a blessing.

not that from Inishmurray.

Many years ago I had suggested that the name *Molaise* may have been compounded from *mo laogh se* as in *Mog* from *mo Aodh og*. In October 1992 on a visit with Terry McGowan to Ballaghameehan, Rossinver, county Leitrim, the home of the O'Meehans, coarbs of St. Molaise, he showed me a site saying that it was St. Mog's church. Molaise is an enigma. In the various *Felire* we find at least seven different people named Molaise, all but one of them in the north Sligo, north Leitrim, south Fermanagh and south Donegal areas. The exception is Molaise of Leighlin, county Carlow. Tradition on Inishmurray would have Molaise of Inishmurray to be the same as Molaise of Devinish in Lough Erne. The coarbship of both was the same – the O'Meehans of Ballaghameehan (see below regarding the *Soiscéal Molaise*). Proponents of the Devinish Molaise would, in general, have him particular to Devinish and would not equate him with Molaise of Inishmurray. The feast of Molaise of Inishmurray is given as 12 August and of Molaise of Devinish as 12 September. In both cases it is the twelfth and they are adjacent months. Molaise's wells and small early Molaise's churches are found in many parts of north Sligo – Ballintrillick, north Leitrim – Kiltycahill, and there is a townland and parish of Lickmolassy in southeast Galway. Ahamlish in north Sligo is *Ath Molaise*. Lough Erne is but a short distance from north Leitrim and in both cases the saint is associated with an island. Also, we find a Molaise in Leighlin, county Carlow, and a church of St. Mog in the home town, Ballaghameehan, of the O'Meehans – coarbs of our Molaise (or Molaises). All this is intriguing and suggestive that there may have been but one Molaise who had some association with Mog. It certainly begs further research.

On Inishmurray the *Soiscéal Molaise* – the Book Shrine of Molaise – was referred to as Molaise's Book. The tradition was that if one were accused of a crime the ultimate test of guilt or innocence was to swear while holding the Book in one's hands. If the accused was guilty then the Book fell from his or her hands. George Petrie, the antiquarian, recorded an occasion in Sligo in 1835 when a court had to be postponed until the *Soiscéal Molaise* was produced as one party objected to swearing on the Bible (Stokes 1868, 276-277). The story told on Inishmurray was that in 1880 an islander accused of some misfeasance travelled, in those times that meant having to go on foot, to Ballaghameehan to swear on the Book but by that time the Book was no longer there. The *Soiscéal* had been accquired by the Royal Irish Academy in 1860\1861 at a cost of £45. The money was raised from Academy members and public subscription. The Academy purchased it from The Rev. Alexander Smullen, who had purchased it from Charles Meehan of Lattone, Ballaghameehan. I am indebted to Miss Aideen Ireland for many points of information gleaned from various Academy minute books. Smullen was the incumbent at Ballaghameehan from 1854 to 1862. There is no basis for Raftery's claim (Mahr & Raftery, 1941, 121) that the Catholic Bishop of Kilmore was involved in the transaction. Its name, *Soiscéal Molaise*, would be consistent with its having been referred to as "The Book" on Inishmurray. The *Soiscéal* did not contain a book at the time it was acquired by the Royal Irish Academy and there is no record of its existence. Rev. Fr. Denis Molaise Meehan on p. 23 of his booklet on Inishmurray has a tantalising suggestion, based on oral tradition of the early 1950s, that a Manorhamilton auctioneer auctioned off the book, sometime in the late eighteenth or early nineteenth century, and that it may still exist in some private library. Furthermore in a postscript appendix Fr. Meehan wonders if the last coarb, who sold the *Soiscéal* to Charles Meehan, should be sought in Derrynahimmerk (*recte* Derrnahimmirk) townland.

It is now in the Royal Irish Academy collection in the National Museum of Ireland and is a beautifully designed work of art. It measures 14.75 cm by 11.7 cm by 8.45 cm. (5.25 by 3.25 by 4.5 inches). The best references to it are those by Raftery (in Mahr & Raftery, 1932, 1941, reprint 1976 – the illustrations in the 1976 edition are reduced somewhat from the 1:1 of the original – pp. 119-121 with plates 57 & 58), and by Raghnall O'Floinn (in *Treasures of Ireland: Irish Art 3000 B.C. – 1500 A.D.*, Dublin 1983, 60, 161-163). O'Floinn describes it as a composite piece of metalwork, dating to the later eighth or ninth century, the first quarter of the eleventh century and the fifteenth century, and notes that it is the earliest of the eight surviving bookshrines. A photograph of it was used on a Christmas card in the late 1980s by both UNICEF and the Royal Society of Antiquaries of Ireland.

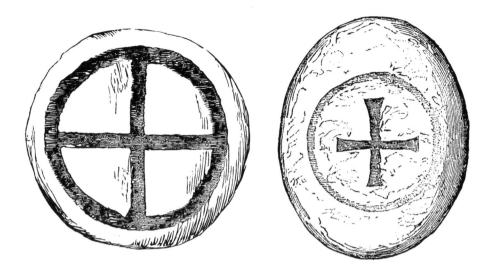

Drawings by Wakeman showing details of two of the inscribed stones.

The inscription on the *Soiscéal* reads, in translation, "A prayer for Cenfaelad the successor Molaisi, under whose auspices was this shrine made complete, and for Gilla-Biathin, the wright, who made the ornament." Cenfaelad was Abbot of Devenish from 1001 A.D. to 1025 A.D. The *Soiscéal* was kept at Ballaghameehan and associated with Inishmurray, again suggesting that the Molaise of both places was the same person. The late Rev. Denis Meehan, whose father was one of the traditional Meehan coarbs of Molaise and who resigned the Chair of Classics at Maynooth College in 1959 to become a Benedictine monk in California, has written a minutely researched book *Molaise of Inishmurray,* published by the *Kerryman* in 1989. Fr. Meehan took the name Molaise in religion when he joined the Benedictine Order. He convincingly argues that Molaise of Devenish and Molaise of Inishmurray are one and the same person.

Richard N. Bailey, "An Early Irish Carved Stone in Northern England", *Journal of the Royal Society of Antiquaries of Ireland*, Vol. 120 (1990), 126-128, has published a further Inishmurray find in the Alnwick collection. This is a circular water-rounded sandstone, 75.2 cm (29.6 inches) across and 14 cm (5.51 inches) high. There is a small depression in the centre of the complicated cross design with an elaborate pelta-shaped ornament filling the spaces between the limbs of the cross on the curved top of the stone. This stone is surely one of the Inishmurray *Clocha Breaca.* Bailey argues that there is no justification for the claim in the *Alnwick Catalogue* (Collingwood-Bruce 1880, 134-135, No. 741) which attributes this stone to Northumbria. He sees Roger Chambers Walker of Rathcarrick as being accountable for its being there.

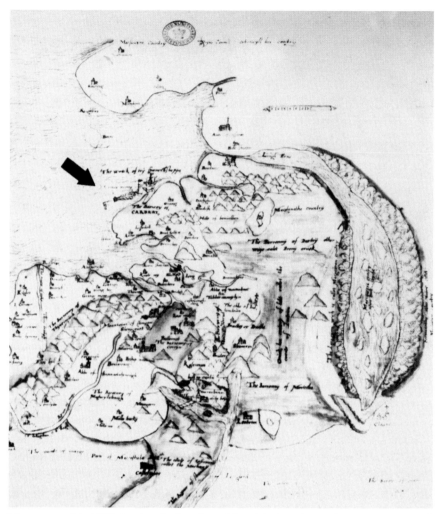

Map engraved in 1589 showing the location of Spanish Armada wrecks and "Inus-Murre" (indicated by an arrow) off the wreck area.

Settlement and Re-settlement

The monks continued to live on Inishmurray until the early twelfth century. O'Dowd of Tireragh was, up to then, suzerain Lord of the seacoast from Killala in Mayo to Bundoran on the Leitrim-Donegal border. But in the early twelfth century the O'Connors, until then an inland clan, pushed out to the sea at Sligo cutting off O'Dowd's lands lying to the north of the Garavogue River. This left Inishmurray facing a "foreign power" on the opposite shore, and so the monks of Inishmurray returned to the land of their allegiance at Aughris in Tireragh, county Sligo and the island was later re-settled by O'Connor protagonists and the secular natives who accepted the O'Connor regime. Exactly when the first lay or non-monastic inhabitants came to Inishmurray is impossible to say. It would appear that there were none on the island in Colmcille's time. Except for a reference to the burial of Moyleen O'Dalaigh (O'Donnell) in 1612, there is, apart from some unimportant references in the Annals, a great silence about Inishmurray until 1653. In that year William Petty carried out Cromwell's survey of the country. The number of inhabitants on the island, referred to as "Inismores", is given as only three persons. This is a most improbable number and may have arisen in one of two ways. Either the enumerator took the easy way out by asking some local for information, or if he did make the troublesome crossing to the island, the inhabitants, save three, hid themselves as well they might in post-Cromwellian Ireland. I tend to accept the first explanation.

The next written reference to Inishmurray occurs in 1779 when the intrepid Dutch archaeologist Gabriel Beranger visited the island.[1] He, fortunately for later generations, was more interested in people than in artefacts and sites – the remains being still there, while the people are gone. He reports only five houses on the island, portending a decline which is certified by the next commentator in 1802. Beranger gives the number of inhabitants as thirty-five, noting that the only English-speakers were a few of the older people. Still more interesting is the islanders' claim, recorded by him, that their lands had descended from father to son for 700 years: that would be since 1100 A.D. This figure is entirely in accord with the date that the monks left the island.

The next commentator on Inishmurray is James McParlan, who made a detailed report on county Sligo for the Royal Society in 1801-1802. He tells us that there was only one family then living on the island (number of persons not recorded) and that they, particularly the grown-up daughters, were most anxious for others to come and live there. He does not give the name of the family, but local tradition records it as O'Currid, a family which was still found on the island after its subsequent re-settlement. It is at this stage that the modern and verifiable history of Inishmurray begins.

Inishmurray, which with the rest of north Sligo had been granted to Sir Thomas Stafford in the early seventeenth century, was now owned by the Hipsley and Sullivan estate. This was a relatively small estate wedged in between the Gore-Booth and Palmerston estates, but it had one advantage over both of these larger estates, namely a large proportion of good bog. When in 1918 there was major agitation for turbary rights among the Palmerston (by then Ashley) tenants, ably guided by the patriot priest Fr. Michael O'Flanagan, a final solution was reached by giving these tenants the right to one-quarter acre (0.10 hectares) of bog on the Hipsley-Sullivan estate. The Inishmurray islanders, by virtue of being actual tenants of the said estate, were each given the rights to a full acre (0.4047 hectares) of bog, rights they still enjoy. However, back to the story of the settlement of the island. At the beginning of the nineteenth century Inishmurray was almost deserted. And the owner of the estate sought the help of Owen Wynne of Hazelwood to solve the problem. He was a remarkable man who has scarcely been given due recognition for the social and agricultural advances for which he was responsible. He was a dedicated farmer; the proper and beneficial use of the land meant more to him than anything. He used nine different types of plough on his own land and had received first prize at Ballinasloe Fair in 1810 for a plough designed by himself. It is not surprising that his advice was sought by neighbouring estates.

He solved the depopulation of Inishmurray in the following way. Tadhg O'Heraughty, a tenant of Gore-Booth, farmed a reasonably-sized holding in Ballycon-nell, Maugherow.[2] Owen Wynne approached his heir, Domhnall O'Heraughty, with the proposition that in exchange for his land in Ballyconnell he take the whole of Inishmurray. Domhnall was not a ready taker and tried to parry the offer as best he could, but both men knew that as a tenant Domhnall was in the weaker position. One of Domhnall's objections was that he would not be able to find a wife to live in isolation with him on the island. But the adroit Wynne was prepared for this, and had obtained the agreement of Margaret McNulty, a cook at Hazelwood, that she would marry Domhnall and go to the island with him. With this and some minor objections overcome, Domhnall had little choice but to accept the offer of Inishmurray.

Margaret and Domhnall were married and some time later, probably in 1802, they left for Inishmurray. Domhnall took a partner, Seán Brady, who with his wife was allotted a holding in the eastern central part of the island. The custom of granting lands either permanently or temporarily to a helper was quite common in Ireland at the time. Such temporary allotments on Inishmurray in the following years are evidenced by field names: *"Páirc Mhic Ruadh"* – "Red Mick's Field", *"Fál Ui Réagáin"* – "the enclosure or field of O'Regan", and *"Garraidhe Sheáin 'Jack'"* – "Sean's Jack's field".[3] All the twentieth century holdings on the island can be traced to Domhnall Heraughty and Seán Brady. One partial exception to this is the O'Currid holding which was purchased by Domhnall's daughter-in-law, after her remarriage, as a dowry for one of her daughters by the second marriage.

On a clear day one can see that on the opposite mainland at Ballyconnell the fields are laid out in rectangles and squares. This was done by, or on the instruction of, landlords when they took over land, up to then generally unfenced or irregularly fenced, from native holders. It was known as squaring the land and made for more varied use and facilitated better drainage. Those particular fields were pointed out as the farm Domhnall Heraughty had exchanged for Inishmurray in 1802.

The population of Inishmurray increased gradually. A sketch drawn in 1836 shows fourteen houses (or seven houses with outbuildings) located in a group south of Cashel, all facing southwest. The census of 1841 lists sixteen houses and a population of eighty-five (forty men and forty-five women). Ten years later the number of people on the island had declined to fifty-three (twenty-seven men and twenty-six women) as a result of the famine. The population of Inishmurray reached its peak in 1880 when there were 102 people living in fifteen houses.

Mary Donlon demonstrates how barley was ground on a stone quern in 1901. This was normally a man's job.

CHAPTER 5

The Island Economy

The new "colonisers" of the island would have had a mode of life comparable to
the mainland peasants. They were subsistence farmers but as seafood was easily
available, they were able to obtain a modest return from fishing and seaweed collecting.
They may, indeed, have been somewhat more affluent than their mainland neighbours. The evidence, however, indicates that the new inhabitants of Inishmurray were
an agricultural people transferred without appropriate tradition into a seafaring
situation. They were Irish-speaking and while the names used for housing, land, and
farm implements and needs continued to be Irish, there were practically no Irish names
for the various parts or requirements of boats. These names were English: tafts were
"tafts", sails were "sails", oars were "oars", rowlocks were "rowlocks", and so on.
Likewise in fishing, the names, with the exception of the *snath breaca* – the thread
used to tie on the bait, were English: "rod", "line", "sink', "bait", and so on. When
trawling from a boat, the square of wood around which the fishing line was wound
was called a "*crannóg*" an Irish word, but this meant a frame and was equated with
the framework needed to build a *crannóg* in a lake. For the first thirty or forty years
on the island the new residents rowed their boats, and sailing only gradually developed
– further evidence for the lack of a seafaring tradition. An old man told me that he
had seen the "quilt" of a bed used as a sail. Indeed it was only the generation who
grew up at the end of the nineteenth century who learned to "cut" sails and even in
the early twentieth century, the islanders often got Mullaghmore seamen to cut sails
for them. The islanders' lack of fishing skill is also shown by the fact that some time
in the mid-nineteenth century a government agency sent a man named John Duthie
to teach the islanders the best methods of fishing.[1]

The islanders kept cattle and sheep and some had horses.[2] Most male and a
considerable number of heifer calves were slaughtered and contributed to a good
protein diet for the inhabitants. In later years families sold from one to four cattle on

the mainland each year to supplement their income. The transporting of cattle to the mainland was a skilled procedure. The cattle were shipped from the mouth of Classey Giolla Phádraig at low tide or sometimes from the quay on the eastern end of the island at about half tide. Animals were made to fast for twenty-four hours before being transported. The centre taft of the boat, usually of an 8.5 to 9.14 metres (28-30 feet) keel, was removable so that cattle could be more easily loaded. The animals were carefully walked down to the water's edge where the boat was lying on its side. A sheeting of boards was laid over the inside of the boat and this was covered by a considerable quantity of straw. Straw was also spread on the rocks where the cattle stood. Ropes with special loopings were placed around the animal's four legs and with one person holding the head and others pulling on the ends of the ropes, the animal was brought gently to the ground. Its feet were then secured and tied by adjusting the loops and it was lifted over the gunwale of the boat. Someone sat on the taft and held its head in a comfortable position. Two and sometimes three cattle would be taken in one boat. The cattle boats always went to Streedagh on the mainland because it had a sandy beach. The boat was run up onto the beach, tilted to the side on which the animal's legs pointed, the ropes loosened, and then the beast simply walked out onto the sand. A suitable day was always chosen, and cattle were allowed a few days to recover on the land of some friendly mainlander before being offered for sale.

Butter-making played a small part in the economy in the days of Ireland's butter markets. Two Inishmurray holdings were able to produce enough homemade butter to sell their surplus in Sligo town. They also sold eggs on the mainland.

Fishing was important to the island economy but had its limitations, the main one being the difficulty of getting fresh fish to market. Hence fish that could be cured, stored, and sold over a period of time on the mainland were more profitable and sought after. These included pollock, ling, wrass (connor or "*bollain*" as it was known on the island), and to a lesser extent, mackerel and herring. Most fish were sold at Grange Fair. The short summer lobster-fishing season was the most remunerative, although the islanders earned little enough. I was present in the early 1930s when an island man was paid three shillings and six pence (17½p) a dozen for his lobsters. Five shillings (25p) and certainly six shillings (30p) per dozen was a good price in those days. It is hardly surprising that at this price, lobster was sometimes used as bait when fishing for *bollain* (connor or wrass). Crab was generally used as bait. At neap tide, a piece of fish, usually a head, was attached to a fishing line and thrown into a sea lough. Small crabs would cling to the fish and be drawn in with the line. When the men caught herring around Inishmurray it was essential to get the catch to Cloonagh on the mainland as quickly as possible. Otherwise it would be a complete loss. Stormy weather and rough seas often prevented this. So during seasons when herring was to be found near mainland ports, the islanders temporarily migrated to such ports – Killybegs, Sligo, and Culleenamore – and fished. Thus they could market the catch fresh. But while living on the mainland they had to pay for everything they needed, unlike on the island where anything might be borrowed from a neighbour, perhaps on a "permanent loan".

Other sea products contributed to the island economy. Carrigeen moss, known on Inishmurray as "*fúdar*", was picked, bleached, dried, and sold in Sligo. *Crannach* (called *miobhan* in the south and, sometimes erroneously, dilisk) grew on the small black shells on the rocks. It too was picked, dried, and sold on the mainland.[3] Some seaweeds were eaten. One mixture of seaweeds and limpets boiled together was called *cruasach*. But the most important sea-based industry was the making of "kelp" from seaweed, especially for those with a fit and reasonably large family to work at seaweed gathering and the burning and transportation of the kelp. Iodine was the chief end product. Sea rods were gathered in winter and dried on low stone walls. Wrack was collected in May and dried somewhat as hay by spreading it out to dry – "lapping" – and finally building it into cocks. The collecting of the wrack was well organised. There were two traditional stewards, who divided the "block" of wrack between the claimants and who, for their trouble, got an extra "half-share" each. Towards the end of June the kelp was burned. First a rectangular stone hearth about 2.5 metres long by one metre wide (8 feet by 3 feet) was built. Turf was placed on this hearth and lit. Once it was burning well, the dried wrack was laid over it. And when this in turn had been lit, the sea rods were laid on top and replenished as necessary. This process produced an immense volume of thick black smoke and, as it was almost always done on the common beside the school, the lunch-time game of running through the smoke, despite its effect on clothes and faces, was enormously popular with the "school let-out".

Kelp was sold by weight after a test of its iodine content. The addition of some "iron ore" (iron pan) procured locally was not unknown. I remember an occasion when an islander tending a kelp fire dropped his clay pipe, causing it to break. He picked the broken pipe up, knocked the unburnt tobacco into the palm of his hand, and philosophically tossed the fragments of his pipe into the fire, mumbling "that will put weight in it". The kelp fire burned for most of the day, and when eventually the hearth had taken all it could hold, the fire was allowed to die down and the molten mass mixed with long sticks into a homogeneous substance. Before it hardened, it was cut into sections – as one would do with homemade toffee – that could be carried with reasonable ease. It was later taken by boat to Mullaghmore where an agent bought it. The kelp trade was eventually eclipsed by the discovery of Chile saltpetre, from which iodine was more easily and economically extracted. Nevertheless during World War I prices of up to £20 per ton were obtained for kelp, and the industry struggled on into the early 1930s.

Other natural resources were harvested for use in cures. The island's "doctor" in my time was the much-beloved Crimley, who was also the island wit. He treated burns with an application of a green freshwater alga known as *conur*. When applied to the burn it set as a firm, occlusive dressing. Its effect was similar to that of

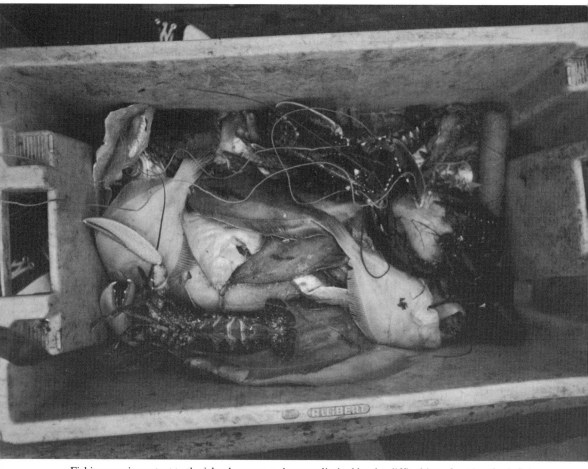

Fishing was important to the island economy, but was limited by the difficulties of getting fresh fish to market. Carrigeen moss, and the extraction of iodine from kelp also contributed to the island economy. Below: islanders lifting lobster pots during the 1920s.

commercial tannic acid jellys, the standard treatment for burns from the mid-1930s to 1950. A plaster made of pounded comfrey leaves, which the island boys gleefully pounded with stones, dried into a pliable yet resilient cast around fractured bones.

WHISKEY MAKING

Quite early on the islanders, perhaps inevitably, had discovered an easier and more lucrative means of livelihood than any of the activities mentioned so far. And this was the making of "poteen" (illegal whiskey), although it was never called by that name on the island. It was known as "whiskey" and was distinguished from that which was legally purchased by calling the latter "parlement", that is, whiskey licensed by Act of Parliament. Poteen-making and its sale on the mainland soon became the principal economic activity of Inishmurray. On the mainland, the making of poteen was indulged in by the minor gentry rather than the peasants.

To make whiskey a person needed raw materials, equipment, know-how, and luck or good judgement in order to obviate official intervention. The raw materials used by islanders, in order of preference, were treacle, brown sugar, white sugar, barley, and very occasionally, potatoes. Treacle held first place because the distillation period when using it took only five days – a short "at risk" period. Using brown sugar instead of treacle lengthened the process to seven to nine days. This increased the "at risk" period, but brown sugar had the advantage of being fairly cheap. Using white sugar also took from seven to nine days, but the advantage was its anonymity since the authorities could not licence its sale as they did treacle and brown sugar. Barley was a speciality and commanded a higher price. The "at risk" time was much longer, and the process was usually reserved for winter-time when weather conditions and shorter daylight gave the distillers greater protection from discovery. As soon as they began to "malt" the barley, the law had been broken. Using potatoes was very much a case of "dúirt bean liom go ndúirt bean léithi ..." ("a woman told me that a woman told her that she knew a woman who made beer from potatoes" – an ill-founded rumour).

To make whiskey using barley, sacks of barley were steeped in running water for twenty-four to thirty-six hours. The barley was then spread on an earthen floor and turned every twelve hours with a shovel. It was then dried in a kiln spread on "drawn" straw or sometimes on a sail supported by wattles. The wattles were so arranged that if by accident the kiln went on fire a quick pull of the main wattle would drop the malt and straw to the ground where its mass and dampness cut off the oxygen, thus extinguishing the fire. When dried, the barley was ground in a hand quern. The barley flour was then placed in a special barrel known as a "keeve" with warm water, and the extraction process began. This was allowed to continue for eight to ten hours before the "worth", also known as "barley tea", was withdrawn. Ten to eleven stone (63.50 kg to 69.85 kg) of malt were put into the keeve, and it was stirred with a shovel while the water was added. Once the shovel could "stand by itself" in the mixture, the desired consistency had been reached.

The keeve barrel had a bung hole, tapped by a tin pipe which in turn was closed by a wooden spigot. Fastened inside the bung hole was the "*sparanach*" – a bundle of briars whose purpose was to prevent any solid material from escaping with the worth. The keeve was raised on stones or placed on top of strong stools, and when the spigot was withdrawn the worth flowed into a "keeler" – a tub without ears. The worth was now ready to be used as the raw material for brewing.

In general the brewing process was as follows. Six gallons (27.28 litres) of treacle, five stone (31.75 kg) of sugar, or else 24 gallons worth (109.10 litres), depending upon which raw material was used, were placed into a 40-gallon (181.84 litres) or even larger barrel. Sugar or treacle had to be dissolved in warm water; usually six gallons (27.28 litres) sufficed. By the further addition of cool water, the temperature was adjusted to milk heat (37°C), Baker's yeast, known as "barm", was broken into the mixture directly or else previously dissolved in water at milk heat and added to the mixture.[4] About two pounds (907.2 gm) of yeast were used. If the mixture was not working well, the temperature was kept up by adding warm water. But if one reached a stage where there was a danger of over-dilution, the temperature was from there on maintained by putting in heated stones, much as people did in prehistoric times in the *fulachta fiadha*.[5] To help fermentation various materials were added as "backing". Hops were best, but the "lees" of porter was said to be particularly good with barley. Heather bloom and camomile were also added. The latter may have improved bouquet. When fermentation ceased, the "pot ale" (usually pronounced "pot dale") was ready for distillation. It was only in the late 1920s that the custom of drinking pot ale as a beer began. At first it was regarded as a contemptible thing to do, and "he drinks pot ale" was said in disparagement. Later the habit became acceptable.

The equipment used in making "whiskey", apart from barrels, kegs, jars, bottles, tundishes (tin funnels) and, as required, keelers, consisted of the following: a still with a fitting head, a copper "worm", a "flake", joint sealant, and a "tinkling". The still was made of tin and had a limited life span. Most adult distillers could make their own. At the turn of the century, Inishmurray was visited by John Power of Powers Whiskey. After examining the equipment he, very sportingly, had a copper still and head sent to the island. This was more magnanimous than it may at first seem, since at the time illegal poteen was a keen competitor with authorised whiskey. Fashioning a copper "worm" was skilled work. It required split-second timing, particularly when turning the hot, lead-filled copper tubing. Lengths of copper sheeting, about four inches (10.16 cm) in width, were hammered around an iron crowbar to form a cylindrical tube. A turnip was inserted into one end of this tube and the tube was then filled with molten lead. The open end was stoppered and the tube grasped with wet-cloth protected hands and twisted around a prepared wooden cylinder, usually a tree trunk. This procedure was known as "turning the worm". Each separate turned tube was a "curve", and the worm was made up of three and sometimes four curves. It took about four stone (25.40 kg) of lead for the process. When fashioning the second and subsequent cylinders, the sheet copper was moulded lower down on the crowbar so that it encircled the slightly narrower part of the bar where the end taper began. Thus the slightly narrower tube fitted snugly into the preceeding opening when the worm was being assembled.

It was customary to buy copper sheeting from Belfast. This may have been for two reasons. In pre-Border days much of north Sligo's trade was with Belfast. Moreover, purchasing the copper in Sligo, the Divisional Police Headquarters, might have aroused unwelcome suspicion. The copper worm was a highly valued piece of equipment and while every dealer would have a still, only three or four people had worms which they lent for a charge as required. Tin worms were sometimes used but they were thought to produce an inferior whiskey. They were square in cross-section, made in one piece, and soldered along the edge.

The "flake" was the barrel into which the worm was fitted. It was filled with cold water to condense the steam into a distillate in its passage through the worm. The flake was placed next to the fireplace on which the still rested. The worm was set in a light frame so that the distillate flowed evenly from the upper opening of the worm, where it joined the arm of the still-head, to the lower opening that protruded from an aperture at the bottom of the flake. It flowed from this pipe into a tundish which conveyed it into a keg. A thick mixture of oatmeal, flour, and water, known as "closing", was used to seal all joints between the still and head as well as the joinings of the worm, the plug of the still, and the aperture in the flake from which the spirit came out. A "tinkling" was a small metal container shaped like a mustard tin. In fact, mustard tins were often used. Visitors who came to wish the manufacturer luck were given a sample taste of the brew in this container.

The entire process from brewing to final distillation was known as "making a throw". Each separate distillation was known as a *lacht*. There were usually three *lachts* in each throw. The product of the first distillate was known as "singlings". All singlings were put back into the still and re-distilled. The product of this second distillation was known as the "doublings", the final spirit. Occasionally a perfectionist would double distill his whiskey to further strengthen and flavour it. The first of the distillate was offered to the "good people" or fairies. It was poured on a clean stone, while the pourer chanted "*Síogaí, Síogaí*" ("Fairies, Fairies"). At the time the doublings began to run, visitors arrived with uncanny precision and were, of course, treated with a shot from the tinkling. This portion, the first of the doublings, was known as *scaithín garbh* ("rough fraction") and was much appreciated by connoisseurs. It was a man's drink.

It was crucial to stop distilling before the unwanted part of the distillate, "the

Still, flake, tundish and keg in the process of making whiskey (it was not known as "poteen" on Inishmurray).

fains", came over. The test was to throw some of the spirit on the still and apply a lighted candle. When the spirit failed to light on the shoulder of the still, it was time to stop. The residue left in the still was the burnt beer. Of course, at the doublings stage there was practically no residue.

The whiskey was then put in kegs and hidden on the island, later to be taken to the mainland on a prearranged night and sold to established retailers. When the whiskey was properly hidden, the Revenue searcher never had a chance. Raids by the authorities on Inishmurray, with one notable exception in my time, achieved little. The spirits were usually hidden in the deep *cladachs* or boulder shorelines. The stones about hiding places were marked in the process, but to prevent its detection stones were thrown all around so that marks were everywhere. The hiding place was marked by aligning two fixed points on either side – as done in marking at sea – an extension of the method of parallax. When burying material in the ground, a deep cut with a long knife was made in the sward so that the grass would not wither when the sod was replaced. For many years during the Troubles there was practically no interference with the trade and the makers became careless. Then, on the early morning of 31 May 1923, a combined party of *gardaí* and military landed unnoticed. Three islanders were caught, either with the contraband in their houses or front gardens. They were arrested, taken directly to Sligo, and at a special court, were given three months' imprisonment. Two of them were fined £25 each and a third £50 with the option of serving a further month for each £25. No fines were paid and the men served their full sentences. After this raid precautions were better observed and the success of the authorities declined, although their interception of the "exported" product on the mainland was occasionally effective.

From 1924 onwards the brewing barrels were buried deeply in the ground. Concrete was laid around the top of the barrel, the lid was put on, and the whole covered by camouflage material. After use, the top was left open for airing but on one occasion this was overlooked and the barrel discovered by Revenue raiders. Four strong young men did their best to smash the barrel but succeeded in breaking only a few staves. A few hours after the party had left the island, the owner had the barrel overground, repaired, and in due course, secreted in another location. I do not believe he had ever heard the principle of Archimedes ennuciated but he was a practical man.

Some families reinvested their capital and did quite well out of the poteen trade. Others only made their quota when funds were especially low. The illegal whiskey trade declined only with World War II and the introduction of sugar rationing. The difficulty the islanders then experienced in obtaining raw materials, principally sugar, and the resulting drop in income was a major factor in the desertion of the island.

A fragment of a millstone, found at *Lochán an Catha*, is now in Sligo Museum; another fragment of it is lost somewhere on the island. As there would have been insufficient water power to drive it on the island it was probably brought out as an anchor and lost on the shore.

The photograph was taken *c.* 1923, possibly by Fr. Brian Crehan, Catholic curate of Grange from 1916 to 1923, as only a clergyman would be allowed take the statue out of *Teach Molaise*. According to Fergus O'Farrell, the statue was originally painted.

The group of island school children are from the three families whose houses were next to the cashel. The group are, from left to right: front row – Domnick Harte, James Harte, Michael Waters, John Harte, John Andrew Waters; middle row – Mary Ann Waters (wife of the King), Elizabeth Heraughty (school teacher and mother of the author), Henry Brady, Paddy Heraughty (author); back row – Martin Heraughty (brother of the author), Paddy Waters, Mary Heraughty (sister of the author).

Social Life and Customs

An account of customs in Inishmurray must begin with religious practices. It appears from as far back as tradition goes that the island people went each Sunday to St. Molaise's house within the cashel to pray. When the late Monsignor John Hynes was curate in Grange, he arranged for the rosary to be recited there each Sunday morning at eleven o'clock to correspond with Mass time on the mainland. One of the older island men, a native speaker, was appointed leader. Eventually the duty fell to my mother, as teacher in the island. This often meant that most of the school children and a few adults would gather with her for the recitation of the rosary. Others came individually during the day and, of course, there were some defaulters. In addition to Sunday's religious observances, there were the stations and visits to holy wells which an individual could undertake at any time of year as well as the "Big Station" on 15 August.

The curates from Grange and Cliffoney on the mainland came once a year, usually in May, to say Mass and hold a station, thus giving many people who might not have been on the mainland for over a year the opportunity of religious observance. The islanders were, of course, all Roman Catholics. It was considered a privilege to go to Streedagh to take the priest and his vestment box containing the sacred vessels and priest's vestments back to the island. This honour was reserved for that year's station holder. As with the stations held on the mainland, each household held the station in turn and if for any reason the householder was unable to accept the station, it was held in the school on his or her behalf. Father Brian Crehan, once curate in Grange, always came on St. Molaise's day (12 August) as well. He was a keen Gaelic scholar and very interested in island traditions.

As elsewhere in rural Ireland there were wakes, but in Inishmurray only those of old people were regarded as appropriate occasions for wake games. One such game was *chugat* (pronounced "hugat") *an babhta* (pronounced "bowthaw"). The *babhta* was a fairly substantial plait made of straw. A human ring was formed by seating everyone on long benches arranged in a circle. One person stood in the centre of the ring. Who this should be was determined by lot. Those sitting then passed the *babhta* from hand to hand behind their backs. The goal of the player in the centre was to catch a person in possession of the *babhta,* thus placing him inside the ring. The disadvantage of being in the ring was that if you thought someone had the *babhta* and moved in his direction, you were subjected to a smart blow between the shoulders from the person who actually had it, with the cry *"chugat an babhta"* ("the bowthaw to you"). Wakes and their concomitant guessing games were liable to erupt into contentious situations. If such a situation seemed imminent, peace was usually restored by someone quickly calling for a prayer for the dead. This prayer would be continued long enough to cool people off, and remind them of why they were there. Since it was felt to be unlucky to carry an empty coffin in a boat, coffins were made on the island. Indeed, as it was customary in rural Ireland to keep a death habit in the house, it was customary on Inishmurray to also have coffin boards ready in case a death occurred.

As some of the above indicates, the islanders had their superstitions but they were not obsessed by them. Indeed when anyone brought up the subject of fairies with older people, they would probably be given the answer "Ah, they used to be in it long ago, but they are all gone now." Nevertheless, as mentioned above, when poteen making, the first glass of the finished product was poured on a clean stone with the supplication *"Síogaí, Síogaí"* ("Fairies, Fairies"). However I noted on at least one occasion a certain lack of commitment on the part of the pourer who added, "I hope it chokes you." Occasionally, for luck, some of the more faithful thought it proper to throw an iron object at a person leaving on an important mission such as delivering the poteen to the mainland. And it was believed to be unlucky to point at a boat with a finger, so the thumb was always used instead. If a woman was churning and gave away something from the house, she was thought to have given her hard-won butter away. As a young boy I delivered the religious newspaper, *The Messenger,* to various homes on the island. But on one occasion when I arrived at a usually prompt-paying customer's home, I was turned away empty-handed – butter-making was in progress. Elf stones were used to cure illness in cattle. The "elf stones" were kept in a small bag in the house where they had last been used until needed by someone else. The bag contained some quartz pebbles, other stones, a silver coin, a threepenny piece, and a nail. These were soaked in water, and the water then used at the curing rite. The person conducting the ritual always waited until sundown. He usually watched through the byre window to be sure that the sun had gone down. He then sprinkled the water along the back and across the shoulders of the animal in the form of a cross. Another cattle cure involved passing a briar that had grown with two roots in the ground, that is, one that had an adventitious root at its free end, around the body of the ailing animal.

Just as many superstitions centred around economic activities or objects, like a boat or cow, important for economic survival, so other superstitions focused on curing human illness. Most were the same cures as used in other parts of rural Ireland, but one, the cure of head fever, was particularly interesting. The folk theory behind the cure was that the head had opened thus causing pain. The aim of the cure was to reduce the head to its proper size. I witnessed the cure once. The woman who performed it was bilingual and said the prayer partly in English and partly in Irish. First she took her apron-string and measured the circumference of the patient's head. Then she prayed "*Or do Pheadar is or do Phol do tháinig go Roimh anoir* ('Pray to Peter and pray to Paul who came to Rome from the East') and also for the Saint for whom the cure is made." At the conclusion of this and further prayers, she again measured the patient's head and proudly announced that it had gone in an inch. Of course an apron-string is a very adjustable measuring tape. Lady Gregory, *Visions and Beliefs in the West of Ireland*, p. 158, says the cure for a headache was accomplished by the use of a prayer which, though she was given it in Irish, she gives only the English translation. The translation is:

"Charm of St. Peter and Charm of St. Paul,
An angel brought it from heaven.
The similitude of Christ suffering death
and all suffering goes with him into the flax."

It was believed that flax absorbed all sin.

A number of superstitions surrounded animals. It was regarded as very wrong and unlucky to injure a seal. The islanders believed that the souls of persons in Purgatory transmigrated to the bodies of seals and thus they were really human beings doing penance after death. Swans, who occasionally came to the waters off Inishmurray, were also inviolable because they were "the children of Lir".

As a people the islanders were as good but no better than any cross-section of people elsewhere. But if they had one characteristic in common, it was their intensely fun-loving nature. Indeed, they enjoyed the outlandish ideas about themselves held by their mainland neighbours and visitors to the island and many a tall tale was told with seeming gravity. One islander used to take off his shoes and leave them at home when going to meet a strange boat coming to the island in order to create the "correct" impression. It is here that stories of island "kings" come in. The tradition of islands having kings appears to be a nineteenth-century innovation. Royalty came to Inishmurray in the following way. One day a yacht with a party of friends of the Gore-Booths of Lissadell got into difficulties near Inishmurray. They were rescued by Pádraig Heraughty and some of the islandmen. Apparently stocks of liquor on the yacht were more than ample and perhaps the islanders themselves were already supplied with poteen. At any rate, a good night was had by all and sometime during

Above left: two islanders, on the left stands Martin Heraughty, with Michael Waters, " King" of the Island, on the right. Above right: Crimley, the island doctor and storyteller, and his wife Maggie in 1948. Below: a group of the islanders with, from left to right, Paul McCann, Domnick Harte (Crimley), John McCann, the postman to the island, Michael Waters, "King", and John Francis Gillen of Moneygold.

the festivities it was decided that since so many other islands had kings, Inishmurray should have one too. Accordingly, with due ceremony, Pádraig Heraughty was crowned king and his wife Nancy, née Healy, queen. Soon afterwards Pádraig died. When Nancy remarried, she took the "royal" title to her new husband, Seán Waters.

Kings had no power or special privileges. The next king, Michael Waters, Seán and Nancy's son, was, however, the major landowner on Inishmurray having inherited from his mother two-thirds of his stepfather Pádraig Heraughty's holding, one third from his parent's holding, and another third from a step-brother who was drowned as a young man. But "king" was essentially a nickname, just as one of his first cousins was known as "prince" because of his kinship with the king.

There were twelve houses on the island when I lived there. There had been sixteen in the 1880s and only seven at the time the islanders left in 1948. Up to 1924 there were seven different family names: Heraughty, Waters, Harte, Boyle, McGowan, Brady, and Donlon. By 1948 Boyle and McGowan had disappeared – the Boyles left the island and the McGowan family had died out.

As all the islanders were descended from Domhnall Heraughty and John Brady, a blood relationship existed between most of the families but, with one exception, there were no cousin marriages until the 1930s. That exception was a step-first cousin marriage about 1950. In all other cases the wives and sometimes the husbands (hence the introduction of new surnames) came from the mainland. From the late 1920s on, Inishmurray was no longer considered an attractive place to immigrate and so in the 1930s we begin to find cousin marriages – three in number and the relationship in each case was that of second cousins. All marriages took place in mainland churches at Grange, Cliffoney, and Maugherow.

Pastimes on Inishmurray were spontaneous and varied. Without planning, a melodeon might be produced and a dance begun. Half sets were the most popular dances, with "Stack of Barley" next, followed by stepdancing and in more modern times, waltzing, the one step, and the polka. Fixed feasts or festivals were always celebrated with set nights. It was customary for a group to go from house to house with an accordion, dancing and singing in exchange for a suitable reward such as tea, currant bread, cake or some other titbit. On St. Brigid's Eve (1 February), known as *Brídeóg* night, the revellers carried a dressed figure representing the saint. Bonfire night (23 June) was, as elsewhere, celebrated with bonfires. On Inishmurray however there was the added attraction of eating lobsters roasted on the bonfire. Inishmurray tradition always claimed that bonfires were in celebration of the expulsion of the Danes from Ireland. Crimley was the island *Seanchaí* (traditional story teller) and many a night was whiled away listening to his vivid recountings.

When I was a student in St. Nathy's College in Ballaghadereen in 1926 the students were allowed out to a concert given by the singer Gerald Crofts. He introduced one of the songs he sang: "The Stuttering Lovers", as being a folk song from Inishmurray. I asked my mother about this and she told me that Ann Boyle of Inishmurray had "The Stuttering Lovers" in her repertoire and that Hughes, who collected Irish folk songs, had visited Inishmurray and probably heard her sing.

The island had its own ballads and rhymes, some stanzas of which I recall:

"Inishmurray I was born in and English laws disown[1]
We've never yet been conquered, our King he is our own
We keep our own distillery; no taxes do we pay
May the Lord protect my island home that lies in Sligo Bay."

The following is a more drinking song and goes as follows:

"God be with old Inishmurray that lies in Sligo Bay
We drank the brew with praties and we stirred it through the tay
But bad laws turned us down and now we bear the bother
But if your brew is still alive we'd drink it and no other."

Outdoor sports such as Gaelic football and hurling were popular when weather permitted. The hurleys were seldom standard; any odd-fashioned piece of wood would do. However, available replacements of balls had to be on hand since a fairly good puck at any time might result in the ball being lost in the Atlantic. Balls were made out of the thick end of big sea rods which were slowly roasted in the *gríosach* ("hot ash") of a turf fire. This produced a ball which, if it did not get too wet, could stand up to four or five games. In choosing a team, the prospective captain challenged another person to form an opposing team by saying "*bualim ort*" ("I challenge you"). If the challenge was accepted, the reply was "*tigim leat*" ("I accept"). Great effort was put into claiming who said "*bualim ort*" first since that person got the first choice of player. Teams might not be complete and equipment might be substandard but the fun and entertainment was unquestionable. The least expected game of all was cricket. It was introduced by one of the Waters boys who was at school in Dublin. To make up numbers we had, perforce, to co-opt the girls and, when in, we had to loan some, often most, of our team to the other side to provide enough fielders.

Apart from dancing, singing, and storytelling, card games were popular indoor pastimes. The most popular was "Twenty-five" but "Nap", introduced by the R.I.C., and euchre, in which red jacks are the top cards, introduced by a returned emigrant from America, were also played. Cards were left in the house in which they had been used or else destroyed. They were never taken home by the person who brought them. That would have been unlucky.

The inside of McGowan's house, House G on map (see pp. 10-11), in 1901: dried fish hang in pairs on hooks from the ceiling. A quernstone, still in use at the time, rests against the dresser, beside it are a 10-gallon keg and a tin can. There is a porringer in a wallco (a wall cupboard), two single gallon crockery whiskey jars for poteen sit on the dresser. The poverty of the time is evident.

The 1899 school house.

Learning and Law

The first attempt to introduce formal education on Inishmurray was made in 1834. But because the schoolmaster, Mr. O'Brien, was a Protestant, the parish priest at Cliffoney warned the islanders that this was an attempt to proselytise them. The parish priest addressed his warning to Padraig Heraughty, who as chief (principal landowner and subagent of Owen Wynne) of the island, added fuel to fire by forbidding the children of other islanders to attend the school and by sending his own sons to the mainland to attend school at Ballyconnell during the winter months. The school master, who was always remembered on Inishmurray as the "*Máistir Dubh*" or "Black Master", lived in a combined schoolhouse-residence erected for him at the western end of the village. He was a single, jolly man who stayed for two years but never had a pupil. When John O'Donovan of the Ordnance Survey visited the island in 1836, he became angry about the treatment Padraig had meted out to the "jovial schoolmaster" and said that someone should report the matter to Mr. Wynne. Padraig was the son of Domhnall, who had taken the island at Wynne's request, and was on good terms with Wynne. Wynne appeared to expect Padraig to "keep order" on the island. Towards the end of 1836, the *Máistir Dubh* shook the dust of Inishmurray from his feet, and Martin, the son of Padraig on whose land the school had been built, took over the premises as his home.

The next teacher, Miss Harrison, came to the island in about 1855. She had been trained in the Central Model School in Dublin. A school-house was provided for her by adding a room to the eastern end of the Waters' home. She subsequently married Michael Waters, the then king and a step-son of Padraig, and taught on Inishmurray until 1900. She had good relations with influential persons on the mainland but one suspects that she distanced herself from the islanders. She had, of course, as had all teachers at the time, been commissioned to suppress the Irish language. Her efforts in this direction did little to enhance her popularity. In 1899,

Group photograph taken in a boat in front of the National School. Front, from left to right: Patrick Heraughty (author), Elizabeth Heraughty (sister of author), Mary Waters?, ?, ?; middle row: Joseph Scanlon (a visitor staying with his grandmother, Mary Scanlon), ?, Florrie Harte; back row: Mr. O'Connell (the school inspector and father of Col. "Ginger" O'Connell of War of Independence and Civil War fame), ?, Mattie Brady, Mike Brady, Winifred McGwynn, Eileen Bee Heraughty, Christina Heraughty (sister of author), ?. As Christina left the island in August 1921, the photograph must predate her departure.

the present school was built on the eastern end of the island, and in 1900 Miss Catherine Moffatt, later Mrs Finnegan, came to teach there. Father Sexton, the school manager, enticed teachers to Inishmurray with the promise that any teacher who spent two years on the island would get first choice of any vacancy on the mainland. Miss Moffatt was promoted to Mount Temple School in Moneygold in 1902 at the end of her two years and was replaced by my mother, then Miss Elizabeth Cummins. Father Sexton died before my mother's first two years were up but she had apparently already formed an attachment to my father and they were married in 1906. She remained on the island until she retired in 1938. At that time she was succeeded by Miss Jennings of Cliffoney who taught there until 1941. The last teacher on Inishmurray was Miss Cait Gallagher, a native speaker from Donegal, who was highly thought of in the community and remained there until the people left in 1948.

In the nineteenth century school attendance ranged from twenty-five to thirty-eight pupils. In the early part of this century, it would be up to twenty in the winter months as older children who had worked during the summer months would come back to study in winter for one or two years after they had officially left school. Towards the end, the average school attendance on Inishmurray dropped to twelve and just before evacuation in 1948 the number was down to eight. The classes spanned from infants to sixth standard, and it took judicial programming to see that pupils in each class or sometimes each combined class were engaged to their best advantage. On occasions, senior pupils would take charge of the lower classes.

The social relations of the islanders with the local government were simple. They paid no rates because they had no amenities except for the services of the medical officer which were seldom required and almost always paid for. Most of the time the islanders cared for their own illnesses and injuries. Oral tradition, however, attributed their exemption from rates to the fact that a local dog belonging to Martin Heraughty once saved a Royal Irish Constabulary (R.I.C.) officer from drowning. In gratitude, it was said, the government remitted the islanders' rates. It is much more likely that Mr. Wynne or Colonel Irwin of Beltra, who developed an interest in the islanders and helped them in many ways, obtained this reasonable exemption for them. When the Irish Free State was established in 1922, officialdom apparently decreed that all citizens should be treated equally so the fortnightly post bag arrived unduly full of rate demands. Crimley's apt comment was *"M'anam do Dhia is do Mhuire* ('My soul to God and Mary') rates from Robinson Crusoe."

The first Royal Irish Constabulary station on the island came about in an attempt to stop poteen making. The first R.I.C. sergeant was William Henry Joyce who arrived on the island in 1837.[1] He moved into Pádraig Heraughty's house after Padraig's death and it became the R.I.C. station for the island. The number of officers varied from as few as two to as many as five, but generally consisted of a sergeant and two constables. It could be argued that the coming of the R.I.C. had a beneficial effect on the island's culture. The members of the force had so little to do, they apparently became avid readers. They brought or had sent to them a good supply of books and interested many islanders in reading, with the result that one could often be surprised by an islander's chance reference to some little-known historical or geographical fact. One would then be told, "I read it in the barracks," or "My father (or grandfather) read it in the barracks." The force also achieved its main objective, that is, controlling poteen making. When the trade had been stopped, the force was withdrawn to the mainland. but as soon as it became apparent that poteen was again being made, they returned to the island station. This was repeated on four separate occasions.

From the beginning the R.I.C. were on good terms with the inhabitants, each group recognising and accepting that the force had a job to do. One incident, in this regard, is worth recording. On this particular occasion there was only one sergeant and a constable. The sergeant was very knowledgable about cattle and was the chief adviser to the islanders in veterinary matters. The constable was something of a martinet. A tentative proposal to the sergeant that it might be no harm if "a little drop" for home consumption were made, was favourably entertained, but provision had to be made for the constable's unyielding sense of duty. A plan was developed. The first move was to arrange a falling out between the constable and an islander whose cattle byres just happened to be located some hundred yards from his dwelling house. Soon the parties were no longer on visiting terms. Subsequently, the man's cow became "ill" and the sergeant was consulted. The cow was housed and part of the directions for its cure was that all mashes and food be boiled in the byre. There is no record of the cow's reactions, but what was actually taking place was the brewing and distillation of the "drop". To his credit the constable did become suspicious, but the sergeant used his authority to prevent "unnecessary" investigation.

The R.I.C. station was manned by volunteers and indeed some members of the force requested posting to Inishmurray at the most frequent permitted intervals. The policing of the island was not continuous, in fact the station, as mentioned, was manned and vacated on four occasions. It was finally evacuated in 1895, at the same date as the Mullaghmore barracks on the mainland. After the R.I.C. had left, the island was policed by incursions of the force at two to three-weekly intervals. The principal objective was to keep illicit distillation in check. The police were conveyed to the island by two sailing boats from Mullaghmore. At Streedagh they took on board a party of R.I.C. personnel from Grange, Cliffoney, and Breaghwy barracks. The boats sailed leisurely along the coast in full view of the islanders. The Inishmurray folk quipped that the Mullaghmore boatmen carried only one oar, used to put the boat about, and if there wasn't enough wind to sail, they waited for it. In 1920 the island was raided by a combined R.I.C., Black and Tan, and British Army party. So great was the terror of the "Tans" that the individual given the task of concealing the copper still head, abandoned it in a field (it was found and confiscated by the R.I.C.), and an island woman, married and living in a house just a hundred yards from her childhood home, declared "I'm going home [to her mother's house] to die where I was born."

On the whole the relationship between the islanders and the R.I.C. remained excellent and if occasionally the islanders lost a round to the police, it was fair enough. The Sligo Independent on 24 December 1897 reported one success: "On Tuesday a part of police under Sergeants Morrain and Finnegan, landed on Inishmurray Island and seized and destroyed 195 gallons [886.47 litres] of wash. The police are to be congratulated on these smart captures." The reference to the plural "captures" refers to a second successful raid they had made on the mainland shore near Breaghwy the previous Sunday. The islanders had favourites among the R.I.C. and it was not unknown for a still that had passed its prime to be purposely left in the right place and sufficient instruction given to the right person to find it. Sometimes a small quantity of finished product was planted to earn credit for the R.I.C. member who found it. I was on the island during a raid in which the only acquisition the raiding party made was a five-noggin bottle of spirit that I had succeeded in conveying to the member left to "guard" the boat. There was no necessity whatsoever to guard the boat, but this member was suspected of "fraternising" with the islanders. I can remember the astonishment of the raiders when the man who had been left behind produced his bottle. Later that day, a friend and I made a survey of the contraband on the island. Apart from equipment, we found fifty-two gallons (236.39 litres) of whiskey, thirty gallons (136.38 litres) of which was badly hidden by island standards. Despite their purpose and being stationed across the water, the "old police" were looked upon almost as members of the Inishmurray community. A similar rapport with the modern *gardaí* was well advanced at the time the island was finally vacated.

The house of the "King", Michael Waters, in ruins, photographed in 1981.

CHAPTER 8

The Evacuation

The islanders finally abandoned their home in November 1948, but events had gradually been leading up to this for many years. There had always been emigration from the island to the United States and Scotland, particularly Glasgow, but people had often returned and re-settled on the island. In each house on the island, either a husband, a wife, or both had been to America or Glasgow. But beginning in the late 1920s and early 1930s emigrants no longer returned. Life was better elsewhere. As young people, singly and in twos and threes, moved away, a shift in the island's population structure took place. Only the older islanders and the very young were left behind. The first obvious effect of this on the economy was that those who remained behind began to use the smaller boats. They were not physically fit to handle or man the bigger boats. Indeed some of the islanders who had migrated to the mainland returned to the island to assist on particularly hard days, such as the day cattle were being taken out.

But the real economic crisis came in 1939 with World War II which affected Inishmurray in both small and more significant ways. A motor boat supply service to the island operated by a Killybeg's general store owner, Mr. Gallagher, was discontinued with wartime fuel oil cuts. Fortunately, this was not the island's only means of supply. More importantly, sugar, the basic requirement for the manufacture of poteen, was rationed and it soon became impossible to obtain sufficient quantities to maintain the poteen trade. Furthermore, a number of islanders were lured away by employment in wartime England which was easily obtained and remunerative. Some joined the Irish Army, others the British Army and Merchant Navy. After the war, reconstruction in Britain boomed and wages increased and many Inishmurray lads and lassies then married and settled in England.

During the war years the islanders, guided by their priest at Grange, lobbied the local authority, Sligo County Council, and their local members of the Dáil for a

Above: ex-islanders Margaret Heraughty and her husband John Oglesby in the doorway of their mainland home in Moneygold. Left: Mary Ann Donlon (nee Heraughty), an ex-islander

place to settle on the mainland. In October 1946 the entire Sligo staff of the Land Commission visited the island to inspect conditions and interview the inhabitants. The islanders received a sympathetic hearing, and Sligo County Council agreed to build eight cottages on the coast opposite the island on land the Land Commission had acquired from the late Edward Parkes of Moneygold. The number of island families had dwindled from twelve in 1936 to ten in 1946 and only six by 1948 when the evacuation took place. As a result, only six of the cottages were occupied by ex-islanders. The other two houses were allocated to mainland families. Forty-six people migrated on 12 November, mostly the old and very young. The migration process has gone on. Many of the young children who then came to Moneygold have now gone on to England and the United States. The number of ex-islanders of all ages scattered through Ireland, England, and America as well as those still resident at Moneygold is today about fifty-six.

The land on Inishmurray now lies unused. It is still owned by the previous holders but there is no economic way to use it. A few years after the islanders left, some mainland farmers rented the land and tried to raise sheep there. But they could not get to the island regularly to tend the sheep and the effort was given up after about two years. The arable land is now over-grown by ferns, some over six feet (1.83 metres) tall.

Inishmurray has been officially declared a bird sanctuary and has become a valued observation post for ornithologists. Birds unknown on the island before 1948 have now established themselves. The most important of these are the eider and shell duck. There is also a sizeable tern colony and many passerines – birds who rest on the island on their way to other parts. Ornithologists visit the island in force at least twice yearly in an attempt to control the plague of gulls but also to make counts and observe the conditions of other species and to note any new bird arrivals. At other times, they come alone or in twos and threes to spend a few days observing, recording, and ringing birds.

In the 1960s students from Queen's University, Belfast, spent long holiday periods on the island using some of the then habitable houses. Martin and Joyce Enright (an archaeologist) spent some weeks there in 1980 recording and sketching the cross-inscribed slabs – commendable work as the weather continues to take its toll on the carvings. From 1977 to 1980 a party from the Board of Works, under the supervision of Frank O'Connor of Moneygold, spent several weeks carrying out restoration work on the monuments. Otherwise the island has been left to the shades of the past. Its story ended on a November day in 1948 when, with an east wind, the only wind with which one could sail both to and from Inishmurray without tacking, and which, perhaps symbolically, said "Will ye no come back again," the islanders left their homes for the last time. I do not think they will come back again but "*I lionta Dé go gcastar sinn*" ("Into God's nets may we be gathered").

APPENDICES

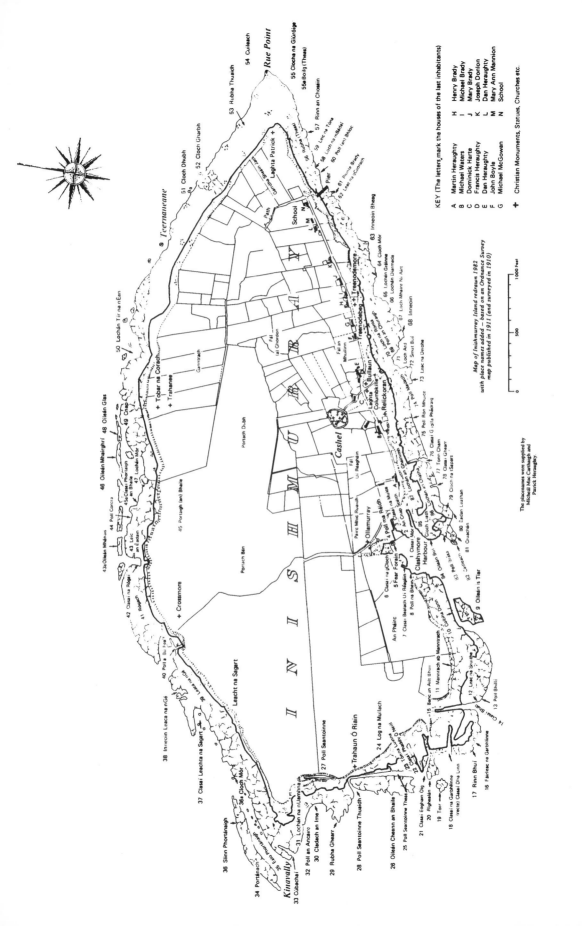

Map of Inishmurray Island redrawn 1982
with place names added – based on an Ordnance Survey
map published in 1911 (and surveyed in 1910)

The placenames were supplied by
Mícheál Mac Carthaigh and
Pairick Heraughty.

KEY (The letters mark the houses of the last inhabitants)

A	Martin Heraughty	H Henry Brady
B	Michael Waters	I Michael Brady
C	Dominick Harte	J Mary Brady
D	Francis Heraughty	K Joseph Donlon
E	Dan Heraughty	L Dan Heraughty
F	John Boyle	M Mary Ann Mannion
G	Michael McGowan	N School
+	Christian Monuments, Statues, Churches etc.	

0   500   1000 Feet

1 Clasaí Mór
2 An Cnap
3 Clasaí Sruth
4 Poll na Réidh
5 Fear Foráin
6 Clasaí na gCloch
7 Clasaí Beatach Uí Réagáin
8 Poll na Bheinn
9 Oileán is Tiar
10 Cartar Donn
11 Manaradh ab Mannitrach
12 Leac na Suirbe
13 Poll Bhuilí
14 Clasaí Bhuó
15 Banc an Áilt Bhuí
16 Fáirteac na Garbhlinne
17 Rinn Bhuí
18 Clasaí na Garbhlinne (recte) Clasaí Dhá Linn
19 Torr
20 Ríghealán
21 Clasaí Eoghan Óig
22 Clasaí O Néill
23 Clasaí O Néill
24 Log na Mullach
25 Poll Saontoinne Theas
26 Oileán Cheann an Bhaile
27 Poll Saontoinne
28 Poll Saontoinne Thuaidh
29 Rubha Ghearr
30 Cladach an Ime
31 Lochán na nUaimhne
32 Poll an Ancaire
33 Cúbachaí
34 Portánach
35 Eas Dúth na gCat
36 Slíán Phortánaigh
37 Clasaí Leachta na Sagart
38a Cloch Mór
38 Innceoin Leaca na Sagart
39 Rubha na gOu Fsst
40 Poll a Bú Fsst
41 Roslach
42 Clasaí na Róga
43a Oileán Mhéanais
43 Leic an Éadan
44 Poll Corcra
45a Clasaí Phórtaigh an Bhaile
45 Portaigh (an) Bhaile
46 Oileán Mháirghirí
47 Lochán Mór
48 Oileán Glas
49 Cnap
50 Lochán Tír na nÉan
51 Cloch Dhubh
52 Cloch Gharbh
53 Rubha Thuaidh
54 Cuileach
55 Cloche na Giúrtige
55a Boilg (Theas)
56 Rubha (Theas)
57 Leic na Tons
58 Loch na mBéast
59 Leic na Tons
60 Poll (an) Bhoc
61 Pointe Brady
62 Leac na gCoinneach
63 Cloch Mór
64 Cloch Mór
65 Lochán Gráinne
66 Lochán Diarmada
67 Loch Mhaire Ní Airt
68 Innceoin
69 Loch na Drothe
70 Poll an Churraigh
71 Loch Ard
72 Srual Buí
73 Leac na Drothe
74 Poll Naoimh
75 Poll Rón Mhuice
76 Clasaí G úlla Pádraig
77 Tonn Cham
78 Clasaí na Sagart
79 Cloch na Leathan
80 Éadan Luathan
81 Cruachán

Teernaneane
Rue Point
Kinavally
INNISHMURRAY
Cashel
Clashymore Harbour
Ollamurray

Tobar na Corach
Trahanee
Crossmore
Leacht na Sagart
Trahaun Ó Riain
Laghta Patrick
School
Treenodemore
Treenodebeg
Bullaun
Laghta Columbkille
Relickoran
Pier
Gurteen
Path
Fál an Mhuilinn
Fál (a) Ghordon
Portagh Dubh
Portach Bán
Párnc Mhic Ruaidh
Fál Uí Réagháin

Language Use and Placenames

The dialect of Irish spoken on Inishmurray was nearer to Connaught Irish than to any other dialect. But Inishmurray native speakers were able to converse easily and fluently with Irish speakers from the Donegal Gaeltacht. During my life on the island, from 1912 to 1935, there were at least eight native speakers. By 1948 when the remaining families moved to the mainland, there was only one. Nevertheless, many Irish words survive in placenames of which a complete list is given.

A number of Irish words used on Inishmurray appear to be unique to the island. *Clugat* refers to pounded wheat boiled with milk. The depressions in the rocks in which grain was husked or pounded were known as *clugat* holes. *Clugat* in medieval Irish meant helmet. A possible association is the practice of medieval soldiers of mixing their rations of meal and butter in their helmets and eating from them. "Recklin" described a series of turf footings joined together to form a continuous line of turves up to four or six yards long. *Turdan* referred to a small clamp of turf. *Scaithín garbh*, the term for the first run of the second distillation when making poteen, is also unique to Inishmurray. A *liomlóg* was a small, rather vicious crab with flattened claws and a purplish hue. The *clabhrach* was the underpart of the crab to which its limbs were joined. *Ag mionnachu*, or the anglicised version "minnaghing", as mentioned in the text referred to a particular kind of crab fishing. A *cailleach* ("old woman", also "nun") was a female crab or lobster: *clearach* ("cleric") was the male crab or lobster. I suspect that both these names are derived from the lobster whose colour might have suggested a clerical connotation. Other unique Irish words include: *bomaragh* – fishing with a float, *culóg* – the second man on an oar (on the Blasket Islands this referred to the hillside into which the gable end of a house was built and could therefore mean support), *mocallaí* – wild rosehips, and *pobail* – wild rhubarb.

Equally interesting are the English phrases and sayings and a few which appear to be derived from the French. On entering a house where the occupants were eating it was virtually mandatory to say, "sit you merry". This is certainly a very English phrase. The phrase "mizzling rain" incorporates an obsolete English word and meant less than a drizzle – an almost visible precipitation or wet fog. The word "munging" on Inishmurray meant eating with relish and may come from the French *manger*. The phrase "to frissie up" meant that a girl would arrange her hair in curls, possibly from the French *frise*. There was undoubted contact between the islanders and smugglers who brought contraband from the Continent, generally from France. This may indicate the origin of such words.

The following is a list of the Irish placenames used on Inishmurray. It was compiled by Mícheál Mac Cárthaigh (McCarthy) and first appeared in the journal *Dinnseanchas*. The numbers correspond to those on the map of Inishmurray. The list of names, beginning with the Harbour or *Clasaí Mór*, follows the shore in a clockwise direction, around the island.

1. The Harbour, or *Clasaí Mór*. A number of deep inlets cut into the rock, and varying in length from about seventeen to one hundred feet (5.18 to 30.48 metres) are known as classeys. The sides are roughly parallel. *Classy Bán,* on the opposite shore, near Mullaghmore, gives Classie Bawn Castle its name. Ó Donovan (*O.S. Letters*, p. 42) writes "*Claisidh Mór*", and Wakeman in 1884 writes it "Clashymore". Nevertheless, the form used here is *clasaí*, cf. Altanaclossagh on the shore of the mainland (*O.S. 25″* sheet LV, 15). The form *clais* is common in placenames on land. In this case the hollows or entrenchments apply to the sea-floor. The word *poll* is applied to the shorter deep inlets.

2. The *Cnap Scéith*. An upward, steep-sided rock, bulging from a broad flat base. *An Cnap Scéithe* "the jutting knob".

3. *Clasaí na Muic*. *Clasaí na Muice* "the *clasaí* of the pig". The reference is to a protruding part of the

rock which resembles a pig's head.

4. *Poll ma Réidh*. At the entrance to *Clasaí na Muice*, on the northern side, is a level area of rock. It measures about thirty yards by twenty (27.43 by 18.29 metres). One may step from there to a ledge lower down and fish in the poll or deep pool. *Poll ma Réidh* "the pool at the level place".

5. The *Fear Forain*. This is a large square rock in fairly deep water. It is not covered at high tide. At ebb tide it has a little beach of large stones, which, through movement in stormy weather, have eroded the base somewhat. Very low down on the east side is a crevice or *cuas* which usually holds a piper lobster. Perhaps this useful crevice gave the rock its name: *farr*, g. *gairre*, a pillar, post, prop; *purrán*, a little crevice. *An Fharr Phurráinn* "the creviced rock"?

6. *Clasaí na gCloch*. "The *clasaí* of the stones".

7. *Clasaí Bealach a Réigin*. *Clasaí Bhealach Uí Réagáin* "the *clasaí* at or near O'Regan's pathway". This is the local interpretation. The surname does not appear on O'Donovan's list of 1836, nor Wakeman's list of 1884. Two fields in the holding, which in O'Donovan's time was owned by Pádraig Heraughty, are known respectively as Upper and Lower *Fál a Réigin*. *Bealach a Réigin* is on the same holding. It was a custom to give the use of a field or fields to a workman employed by the owner.

8. *Poll na Bhéin*. *Poll na nDuibhéan* "the pool of the shags". Shags haunt the rocks nearby, known as *Bun na nDuibhéan*.

9. *Oileán is Tiar*. "West Island" is immediately to the west of the harbour, and possibly got its name from the inhabitants, as they entered or left *Clasaí Mór* in their boats.

10. *Colbha Donn*. "The brown ledge".

11. *Manntrach*. A ridge of boulder clay slopes inland. It is steep and smooth. Its seaward face is known as *Alt Buí* from which a fishing bank in the sea derives its name, *Banc an Ailt Bhuí* (No. 15 below). Immediately behind the ridge is a sheep-pen, *Manntrach*, which gives the ridge its name.

12. *Leac na Sruif*. *Leac na Sruithe* "the rock of the current". The current sweeps past this rock at speed. Where the River Bonnet enters Lough Gill, county Sligo, and causes a strong current in the estuarine

part, the nearby hillside is known as "sriff".

13. *Poll Bhillí*. "Billy's pool".

14. *Clasaí Bhab*. "Bob's *clasaí*". A man named Bob was drowned here. At the landward end, a small cavern having a narrow entrance gives rise to a whistling sound when the wind blows from the south. This is *Poll an Phíobaire* "the hole of the (fairy) piper".

15. *Banc an Ailt Bhuí*. This fishing-bank is about a kilometre and a half out at sea. It takes its name from the seaward side of *Manntrach* (No. 11). *Banc an Ailt Bhuí* "the (fishing) bank of *Alt Buí*"; *Alt Buí*, "yellow cliff".

16. *Fáirleac na Garbhlinne*. This rock is stepped or terraced. From three-quarters to full tide the swell spills over the rock-terraces (the terraces indicate the stratification planes) into *Clasaí Bhab*, and except in very calm weather, it breaks as a wave as it comes over. *Fáirleac na Garbhlinne* "the shelving rock of the rough waters". *Fair* – (for) – means "hyper-, over-, etc."; *leac*, according to Dinneen, may be applied to any sedimentary rock. Dinneen also has *faróg* "a natural terrace on shore or hill", *farragán* "a shelving rocky place, a ledge or terrace".

17. *Rinn Bhuí*. "Yellow point".

18. *Clasaí na Garbhlinne*. "The *clasaí* of the rough waters".

19. *Righealán*. The rock slopes gently from one side to the other. The name is probably from *ríghe* "a slope". Cf. "*Réidhleán*", a level place or area; "Rylane", in place-names (Dinneen, p. 889).

20. Torr Rock. A rock in the sea opposite *Righealán*. It is flat, low, and covered with seaweed. *Torr* "a pile, a heap". *Torrán* "a heap, a pile, a hillock".

21. *Tón na Luinne*. A long smooth rock stretches into the sea. It is almost level, and nine or ten feet (2.74 or 3.05 metres) wide. The sea-end slopes suddenly downwards as a steep ramp. In a strong groundswell the rock splits the incoming waves and a heavy shower of spray is thrown upwards many feet, falls and drenches it. This rock is never submerged, not even by a spring tide. *Lonn* "a heavy swell in the sea"; *tón* seems to refer to the sea-end of the rock (note also *tonn*, "a splash of water" (Dinneen)).

22. *Clasaí Eoghain Óig*. "Eoghan óg's *clasaí*". The descendants of Eoghan óg still bear the agnomen.

The family name is Conway, and it is generally held that this is another form of the name O'Connor.

23. *Log na Mullach.* "The hollow of the ridges".

24. *Clasa Phaddy O'Néill.* "Paddy O'Neill's *clasaí*".

25. *Poll Seantoinne Theas.* This is the southern entrance of a cavern into which the waves rush. (See No. 27.)

26. *Oileán Ceann an Bhaile.* "The island at the head of the town" (i.e., the island of Inishmurray).

27. *Poll Seantoinne.* A cavern almost five hundred feet long (152.4 metres) extends from the shore to an inner lagoon in a S.-N. direction. The waves rise as they advance through the narrow high-walled space, and break spectacularly at the northern exit. *Poll na Seantoinne* is a common name for blow-holes. Speaking of one at Lismuinga, county Clare (O.S. map No. 17), Westropp says: "The Poll-nashantuna is one of those large funnel-shaped hollows, down to an underground stream, or to the sea. The name occurs at several places in North Mayo, notably Downpatrick in Tirawly and in North Mullet" (*J.R.S.A.I.*, XLV, 274). He mentions similar caverns in county Clare. The name occurs in the townland of Kilkinahan in the barony of Bere. Dinneen (p. 1086) suggests that *sean* may be under the influence of *sain* "special, different". This points to a translation as "the cavern of the special wave". Cf. also *son* (p. 1086).

28. *Poll Seantoinne Thuaidh.*

29. *Rubha Ghearr.* "The short point".

30. *Cladach an Ime.* "The flat stony shore of the butter". Butter is believed to have drifted in here as a result of a ship-wreck.

31. *Lochán na nUamhna.* "The *lochán* of the caves". A long stretch of sandstone having a vertical face is severely eroded by the storms' movement of large stones along its base. The caves vary in size; that next to the *lochán* is about thirteen feet square by three or four feet high (3.96 metres by 0.914-1.22 metres).

32. *Poll an Ancaire.* A ship, named the *Margate Knight,* was wrecked here. The anchor still lies in the pool.

33. *Cúbachaí. Portánach* is a long rock of almost three hundred yards (274.32 metres); the channel which separates it from the mainland varies from about twenty-seven to thirty-six yards (24.7 metres to 32.92 metres) across. This channel is slightly serpentine; from N.E., it runs W.S.W., and gradually curves to S.W. At this exit, on the mainland side, the shore-line curves round to form a narrow inlet, some fifty-two yards long (47.55 metres), running N.E., i.e., in the reverse direction. The curve or bend is the most westerly point of the mainland, and is called *Cúbachaí* "the bends or curves".

34. *Portánach.* "The crab place". Crabs are plentiful here.

35. The *Ealó* of *Portánach.* A silent current moves through the channel. There is a danger of being trapped if fishing from certain rocks during the flowing tide. Older people conscious of this, sometimes urged: "Mind the *éaló* of *Portánach*".

36. *Slinn of Portánach.* "The flat of *Portánach*".

36a. *Cloch Mór.* "The big boulder".

37. *Clasaí Leachta (?) na Sagart.* "The *clasaí* of *Leachta na Sagart*" (supra).

38. *Inneoin Leaca na nGé.* "The pilaster of *Leaca na nGé*". A long rock with vertical sides juts into the sea. From one side extends a rectangular buttress, the sides of which are also vertical. This word, *inneoin*, occurs in Nos. 63 and 68.

39. *Leaca na nGé.* "The brow of the geese".

40. *Poll a Bú Fea.* This is a cave where the wave, rushing in, compresses the air to such an extent, that it is forced back through the entrance, blowing spray outwards and upwards. The name seems to be onomatopoeic, *bú* representing the sound during the inward compression, and *fea* that of the outward release.

41. *Rógach. Rógach* is a long, level rock, stretching into the sea. The cracks or joints are at right angles to one another, and to the horizontal bedding planes. The removal of regular-shaped blocks by storms has left it with a number of steps or shelves, on both sides, one above the other.

Rógach may represent *Urógach.* Dinneen equates *uróg* with *urbhac* (*ur* "edge" + *bac* "an angular space, fire-hob, etc"). In the context of the name-form *Rógach,* the reference seems to be to the series of regular-shaped steps; hence "the stepped place". A limestone rock on the foreshore at Bundoran juts into the sea; it has terraces similar to those of *Rógach* and is known as *Rógaí*.

The omission of the initial vowel in *Rógach* and *Rógaí* may be compared with *Oirthircheann Rircheann Rerrin*, translated, and now generally known as, East End, Bere Island, county Cork.

42. *Clasaí na Rógaí.* "The *clasaí* of *Rógach*".

43. *Leic an Eádain.* "The rock-face".

43a. *Oileán Mhanais.* "Mánas's Island".

44. *Poll a'Chorcra.* Sea-urchins at the bottom of the pool give a purple effect to the water. The name is probably *Poll Corcaire* or *Poll Corcra* "the purple pool".

45. *Portaigh (an) Bhaile.* "The village bogs". A bog at the back of the village.

45a. *Clasaí Portaigh (an) Bhaile.*

46. *Oileán Mhairghrí(?).* This name form possibly refers to *maghar*, which, unlocalised, is explained by Dinneen as "sprats, spawn, small samples of anything". Mr. Harte understands that the little island was named after a small fish which was more numerous here than elsewhere along the shore. It has been described as being about the size of a coalfish, of a reddish-brown colour on the back and down the sides. The belly was white or greyish-white.

The name *maghar* appears on lists or names of fishes from Teelin, Downings Bay and various coastal districts in county Donegal (*Irish Naturalists' Journal*, VIII, 424). The fish may be growing pollack.

47. *Lochán Mór.* "The large pool".

48. *Oileán Glas.* "The green island".

49. *Cnap.* This is a hump on a rock floor. "A hump, a knob".

50. *Lochan Tír na Éan.* "The pool of *Tír na nÉan*".

51. *Cloch Dhubh.* "Black boulder".

53. *Rubha Thuaidh.* "Rue North" *(supra)*.

54. *Cuileach.* At the eastern end of the island the rock extends underneath the sea for some hundreds of metres eastwards. This is overlaid by stones and gravel, built up by the waves from the west, which have been refracted along the north and south shores of the island. About two kilometres on either side of

this tombola are two *boilgs, Boilg Thuaidh* and *Boilg Theas*. In ground sea, when these *boilgs* break, a wave from each sweeps in the direction of the tombola, where they clash, throwing the spray upwards from ten to thirty feet (3.05 to 9.15 metres). According to O'Rahilly *(Celtica,* 1, 371) *cuilithe* came to be associated with eddying or bubbling water, under the influence of the phrase *cuilithe guairneain* "whirl pool etc". This would be the condition obtaining towards the tip of the tombola in ordinary non-stormy circumstances. *Cuilitheach Cuileach* "the eddying place".

55. *Clocha na Giúróige.* "The rocks of the tern". It lies beyond No. 54 and is submerged at high water.

55a. *Boilg Dheas.*

56. *Rubha Deas.* "South Rue".

57. *Rinn an Chosáin.* "The point of the footway".

58. *Loch na mBádaí.* "The loch of the boats", also known as *Loch na Ceilpe,* "the loch of the kelp".

59. *Leic na Tóna.* A very slippery rock where the unwary came to grief.

60. *Poll (an) Bhloc.* "The pool or inlet of the blocks". The men of the island were interested in the quantities of seaweed thrown up by the storms in the inlets. It was used in the production of kelp. A mass of seaweed rolled up by the "in-wash" was usually referred to as a block.

61. *Pointe Brady.* "Brady's point".

62. *Leac na gCaorach.* "The rock of the sheep". Sheep for the market were put aboard the boats here.

63. *Inneoin Bheag.* "The little pilaster buttress" or "supporting stone".

64. *Cloch Mór.* "The big boulder".

65. *Lochán Ghráinne.* "Gráinne's *lochán*" or "pool".

66. *Lochán Dhiarmada.* "Diarmaid's pool".

67. *Leac (?) Mháire Ní Airt.* "Máire Ní Airt's flagstone".

68. *Inneoin.* "Supporting stone" or "pilaster".

69. *Port a churry.* Port an Churaigh "curragh landing-place".

70. *Loch na Rónta.* "The loch of the seals".

71. *Loch Ard.* "The high loch".

72. *Smut Buí.* "The yellow snout" – a rock.

73. *Leac na Deibhe.* "The rock of change" (of wind). When the wind changed from north to south, the waves splashed against the face of the rock, making a loud noise. *Deibhe* "difference, variety".

74. *Poll Madadh.* "Otter's pool".

75. *Poll a Rún vick.* A seal is usually found in the pool and the name-form may be *Poll Rón-mhuice*, "seal pool". *Muc Róin* "a seal"; note the omission of final "o" in Nos. 2,3 and 12.

76. *Clasaí Giolla Phádraig.* "Giolla Phádraig's *clasaí*".

77. *Tonn cham.* "The crooked wave". The wave rolls in obliquely across the flag.

78. *Clasaí Ghearr.* "The short *clasaí*". It is the shortest of the classeys.

79. *Cloch na tSapars.* "The sappers' boulder".

80. *Eadan Leathan.* "The broad rock-face".

81. *Cruachán.* This is an eminence on the landward side of No. 82; "the little hill" or "mound".

82. *Cailleach.* The rock to which this name refers is visible until the tide is about three-quarters full. It is difficult to associate it with its name. There is no local evidence that the figurative meanings of *cailleach* are particularly relevant; *Cailleach*, a veiled woman, a hag, an old woman; fig. a stone boat anchor, a female crab, a dogfish, a cormorant, a seashore nymph, etc. It is tempting to suggest that the last meaning is relevant, as there stands, on the opposite side of the harbour, another rock, the *Fear Forain* (No. 5).

83. *Poll Brása.* A rectangular inlet of about eighteen feet by two and a half to three feet (5.49 metres by 0.76 to 0.92 metres) is cut in the rock. It traps dried bits of seaweed, wood, etc. and, in summer-time, jelly-fish. This name may be derived from *práiseach,* figuratively "broken bits"; *Poll Praise* "the pool of the broken bits". Cf. the doubtlets *pras, bras*; *piardóg, beardóg.* Note, however, *braisaidhe* "a sea-bream" (*Irish Naturalists' Journal*, VIII, 346).

84. *Oileán Buí.* "Yellow island".

85. *Cloch Liath.* "Grey stone".

86. *Lochán an Chatha* (?). A flat rock at the harbour-side was used for landing or embarking. Near its centre is a depression, which retains the salt water. It is about three feet deep (0.92 metres). The tradition remains here that a great fight occurred between an invading force and the inhabitants. "The pool of the battle".

87. *Lochán an Ghainimh.* "The lakelet or pool of the sand".

Bomore and its tidal rocks: About three kilometres to the north of the island is a rock called Bomore. It rises some ten or twelve feet (3.05 or 3.66 metres) over the high water mark. The name appears as Boahinshi Rocks in Larkin's map, and it is known locally as Bomoreahinsha and Bomore. "The last is more general" (*OSNB*, Par. Aghamlish, II, 22).

At the western side of Bomore, a rock appears at half tide. As the tide falls further, this rock is seen to be part of Bomore. It is known as *Bo Beag.* Cf. Bowe Veg and Clet y Bowe Veg, "the little tidal rock" and "the isolated rock of the Bowe Veg, in the Isle of Man *(Place Names of the Isle of Man* – Kneen, p. 17); "*bodh*, a rock over which the waves break; from N. *Bothi*, a breaker" (*Norse Influence on Celtic Scotland*, p. 143); "*Bodi*, a tidal rock" (Kneen, *op,cit.*, p. 643, Vol. VI). "Bow Beg Chitterland, a place for white pollocks [little Kitterlandrock]" (*A Manx Scrapbook* – W. W.Gill, p. 92).

Close to *Bo Beag* on the western side is a number of submerged rocks, called *Clochán a dheas* (*Clochán Theas*) on the south side and *Clochán a hoi* (*Clochán Thuaidh*) on the north side. (Cf. Bogha Clachan, Clachan Reef in Rathlin Island, Co. Antrim, s.s. *bogha* "wave, reef", *Irish Language in Rathlin Island* – Holmer, p.1165).

Another placename common to all three islands may be mentioned: Rue point, at the E. end of Inishmurray, at the S. end of Rathlin and on the N.E. shore of Man.

On the western side, Bomore is separated by a *clasaí*, from a tidal rock called *Leic Bhuí* "the yellow rock". At the southern entrance, at low tide, an angular face of Bomore is seen to be covered with *creathnach* (*Rhodymenia palmata* – *Clare Island Survey* – R.I.A. 1911). This is an edible young seaweed which grows on mussels. The face is known as *Leac na Creathnaí.*

Half-way through the *clasaí*, in the middle of

the passage, is a submerged rock awash at three-quarters tide. A current runs through from N. to S. during the flowing tide, along both sides of the rock. The reverse occurs during ebb. A rock lying in a tidal stream causes a reverse flow on its down-stream side; this forms a depression as the water eddies downwards. *Clasaí na Sútaitne* "the *clasaí* of the eddies".

Some distance to the west of Bomore lies another rock called *Seadán*. It appears shortly after the tide begins to ebb. The name refers to the noise made by the water's splashing around it; *ag seadáil sáile* "splashing spray". *Seadán* "the splashing one".

Boilg na Glamhaí. This *boilg* lies between *Seadán* and *Leic Bhuí*. Note *glámhach* "murmuring, noisy"; *glamhán* "a murmuring, complaining" (Dinneen). At night, or in a fog, did the fisherman differentiate between *Seadán* and *Boilg na Glamhaí* by their respective sounds, ie. splashing and murmuring?

The island interior: A short distance to the east of the central north-south axis of the island, and near to its south coast, is a large *caiseal*, roughly circular in shape, and its wall varies from seven to fifteen feet (2.13 to 4.57 metres) in thickness at the base. This is known as "the *caiseal*" and within its wall are the following:

Teach Molaise, "the house or oratory of St. Molaise". It is called after the patron saint of the island, and is the best preserved of the three small churches inside the *caiseal*.

Teampall na bFhear, "the church of the men", is sometimes known as *Teampall Molaise,* and as *Teampall Mór*. According to Wakeman this is considered to be a church, as distinguished from an oratory. Men are interred in the cemetery which surrounds it. The burial ground for women is some distance outside the *caiseal* at *Teampall na mBan*.

Teampall na Teine, "the church of the fire", a structure according to Wakeman, not older than the fourteenth century, has also been known as *Teach na Teine*. The legend exists, that here, of old, burned a perpetual fire, from which any extinguished hearths on the island were rekindled. It was believed that all the island's fires were kindled or relit from *Teach na Teine*.

Within the *caiseal* there are also three beehive cells. One of these, Toorybrenell, is also known as the "school-house". Of this, O'Donovan in *O.S.*

Letters p. 37 dated July 1836, says: "It is called by the natives *Tuar Uí Bhreunail* i.e. O'Brenal's *Tuar* or Tower." In interpreting *Tráthán* as an oratory, he says: "The natives say that the word *Tráthán* signifies a place where the monks sung their *trátha* or vespers. I think, however, that it is a corruption of *Túrran*, and means a little Tower ...

"In this I am borne out by *Tuar Uí Bhreunail*, where the word appears in its primitive form *Tuar*." The following anecdote is of interest: Dominic Harte, the last of the native speakers on the island, died in 1949, aged eighty-six. He related during his lifetime, that his mother had told him that Toorybrenell meant "the virgin's waking-place" – *Tórradh Bhruinnille* – and that she added: "She must have been very well thought of, when the monks allowed her to be waked in there", i.e. inside the *caiseal*. Note, however, the different vowel-sounds in *Tuar* and *Tórradh*.

A second cell is known as *Tráthán an Charghais,* "the Lent Oratory". Tradition says that it was here the monks assembled for vespers.

Teach an Allais. This is a stone-roofed structure abutting on the outside of the eastern wall of the *caiseal*, and shaped somewhat like a horse-shoe. It has an aperture measuring two feet square (0.61 metres square), and it is known as "the sweat-house". It is supposed to have been used in somewhat the same way as the Turkish baths of today. Sites of sweat-houses have been found recently in counties Sligo and Roscommon. There are twenty-five sweat-houses in Sligo, thirty-five in Roscommon, five in Mayo and six in Leitrim. There are four such places in Rathlin Island bearing the name *Tigh Fallais*. They occur too in counties Cavan, Tyrone and Down (*J.R.S.A.I.*, 1890, pp. 165 and 1891, p 589).

Na Clocha Breaca, "the speckled stones". This is the largest of three quadrangular structures – styled "altars" – within the *caiseal*. It derives its name from a large number of stones laid on its surface. They are known as cursing stones or swearing stones. Several of them, according to Dr. Heraughty, are decorated, some ornately.

Teampall na mBan, "the women's church". This has already been mentioned and it is also known as *Teampall Muire*. It stands a little distance to the south of the *caiseal*.

Tobar Molaise. A well named in honour of St. Molaise, it stands close to the *caiseal*. It is covered by a stone-roofed structure. Near the parish church of Ahamlish on the mainland opposite is another well of the same name. Another reference to the name Molaise is found in Pollmolasha on the mainland shore (*O.S. Sligo 25″*, Sheet IV 12 + 8).

Áltóir Bheag, "the little altar", is similar in construction to *na Clocha Breaca*, and has a number of stones on its upper surface. This exhausts the list of the remains in *caiseal* and its immediate vicinity.

Wakeman tells us how, around the shore of the island, and at a more or less uniform distance from one another, there is a number of *leachts* or stations. The *leachts* are of uncemented stones, set in the form of a cube, and averaging about five feet (1.52 metres) in breadth and height. They are surmounted by a miniature pillar, engraved with the figure of a cross. From some of these the stone has been removed. The inhabitants of the island had no particular patron-day, but the station was traditionally performed on 15 August. The rounds were begun at *Teach Molaise*, and, moving clockwise, from station to station, the pilgrims made a circuit of the island. Ollamurray, "*Ulaidh Mhuire*". An *ula*, altar or station named in honour or the Blessed Virgin. This was the third station of the circuit.

Tráthán na Riar. Dinneen gives us two forms: *Tráthán na Riar* "the services" oratory", and *Tráthán na Rí-Ghear* "the oratory of the princes (or good men?)". To the inhabitants of the island who left in 1948, the station was known as *Tráthán Ó Riain*, and by no other name.

Leachta (?) na Sagart. There is a tradition that three priests who had been drowned are buried here.

Crossmore. *Leachta Croise Móire* "monument of the great cross". This station takes its name from a cross which rises from the centre of an altar, standing within the enclosure of a low stone-wall.

Trahanee. Wakeman considers this structure unusual in having a surrounding rampart, unnecessary for the requirements of religious exercises. It may, he suggests, have been mistaken in later times for a station, since an altar called "*Áltóir*" stands at a short distance from it. *Tráthán Aodha*, means, according

to O'Donovan, "Aodh's oratory or station".

Tobar na Córach, "the well of the fair win", is situated close to *Tráthán Aodha*. When during a long period of stormy weather, communication with the mainland was necessary, it was believed that by draining the waters of the well into the sea, the storm would abate. Consequently, the well was known as *Tobar na Córach*.

Laghta Patrick. *Leachta Phádraig* is a station at the eastern extremity of the island. The cross-inscribed up-right stone is missing.

Tobernasool. *Tobar na Súl* – the water of this well was used as a cure for sore eyes.

Treenodemore. *Tríonóid Mhor* "the great station of the Trinity"

Treenodebeg. *Tríonóid Bheag*, "the little station of the Trinity".

Crossatemple: *Cros an Teampaill*. This name was not known in the island in 1949. Its use is attributed to Wakeman, who also called it the Station of Mary. The *teampall* or temple referred to is, according to Dr. Heraughty, *Teampall na mBan* nearby. The cross refers to two sculptured crosses on a small flat stone, which rises from the usual table or base.

Laghta Columbkille: Leachta Cholm Cille. This is an altar or station named in honour of St. Colmcille, and is one of the best preserved of its type on the island. It is the first station.

Relickoran. *Reilig Óráin* "the cemetery of Órán", a contemporary of St. Colmcille. It is similar to those already described and is the second station.

In the past the western part of the island was named *Baile Thiar* and the eastern part *Baile Thoir*, suggesting, in a sense, that *baile* meant the whole island. The extreme western end is now known as Canavalla, *Ceann an bhaile*, the end of the *baile*. The late Dominick Harte when about to walk or stroll, usually said: "I am going over the town".

The eastern part of the island is known as Rue, *Rubha*, a salient, point of land, etc. Part of the north-east is called Terrnaneane, *Tir na nÉan* "the land of the birds", because that part of the island is more frequented by birds than any other part. An adjacent stony field with sparse vegetation is called *Ganntrach* "the place of scarcity".

Notes Compiled from the School Roll Books

The school roll books were as follows:

> January 1867 to 1885
> October 1896 to1908
> October 1908 to July 1920
> July 1920 to July 1932
> January 1932 to October 1948

The teachers were:

1834-1836 Master O'Brien, *alias*, *Máistir Dubh*; he never had a pupil because he was boycotted, under instructions, as he was not a Roman Catholic.

1836-1867 No teacher and no school.

1867-1988 Margaret Harrison of Bunduff, Cliffoney. She married Michael Waters. Michael Waters owned the thatched house to which the school, a slate roofed room, was attached. It had a separate east door. The oldest roll book begins in 1867. For that year four pupils are entered on 11 January. Harry Brady (11 years), John McGowan (16 years), Michael Waters (26 years) and Pat Brady (9 years). Michael Waters had more interest in school than just the books! He attended for 218 days in 1874 but not thereafter. "Crimley" (Dominick Harte) told the story that initially she, Miss Harrison, had her eyes on Dan (Jimmy) Heraughty for whom she cooked fancy buns and had them delivered by Peggy, "Peggy an Ghainimh" as she was from the "Boro" in Maugherow. The upshot was that Dan eventually married the messenger, Peggy. Margaret Harrison lived into the early 1930s. There were exams in Reading, Spelling, Arithmetic, Grammar, Geography and Needlework, though nobody took needlework as there were no girls. The new school was built in 1899.

1900-1902 Catherine Moffat of Cliffoney. She left in August 1902.

1902-1938 Elizabeth Cummins began on 23 September. She married Martin Heraughty on 1 February 1906. These were my parents and their best man was James Mannion.

1938-1942 Bridie Jennings of Cliffoney was next.

She signed her name in Irish and she entered pupils by their Irish names from 1940 onwards until she left on 17 July 1942.

1942-1948 Evlyn (Cait) Gallagher from Donegal, a native Irish speaker, began on 15 October 1942, and stayed until the evacuation.

Details of class and attendance begins only in 1874. During the 1870s attendances ranged from 55 up to 225 days in the year. The first record of girls attending school is for October 1896. All pupils are recorded as being Roman Catholic. Attendances were normally good with many attending on between 130 and 220 days. However, those in seventh class, having reached "summer absentee status", attended on far fewer days.

Holidays were not always taken in the summer months. The school was closed for November and December 1892, a year in which there had been no holidays up to then. The school was often closed when the teacher failed to get back from the mainland due to stormy seas. It was also closed for the annual "Station" on the island in May or June. Bank holidays were not observed!

Several pupils are entered on the rolls who were not island children. These would have been visiting relatives. Occasionally pupils home from school on the mainland attended classes for days that the island school was open. There are cases of pupils being completely absent for one or two years, the explanation being that they were with relatives in Maugherow, particularly Ballyconnell.

In three successive years, 1930, 1931 and 1932 a past pupil of the school obtained Honours Leaving Certificate. They were respectively John Andrew Waters, Patrick Heraughty and Elizabeth Heraughty. One of them, Patrick Heraughty, got first place in Ireland in English. John Andrew Waters subsequently won the Belt of Honour at Sandringham College in Yorkshire.

Notable Visitors to Inishmurray

1779. Gabriel Beranger, a Dutch archaeologist of French Huguenot extraction, visited the island on 24 and 25 June 1779. He made the very interesting report that "only some of the older people on the island spoke English". He gives the population as being 45 or 46, including children, and noted that they lived in five houses. His account was used by Sir William Wilde in *Journal of the Royal Society of Antiquaries of Ireland*, Vol. 11 (1870), 131-136, and by myself in *Ireland of the Welcomes*, Vol. 42, No. 5, Sept.Oct. 1993, 27-33. Beranger's drawing from the island of an ornamented four-handled mether, a wooden drinking vessel, was published by Wilde (1870, 132).

1791. The French Consul, Charles Etienne Coquebert de Montbret, during his two and a half year stay in Ireland, made three tours. Ernst, his nine year old son, was with him all the time. His notebooks are in the Bibliotheque Nationale in Paris and the Museum Library in Rouen. Síle Ní Cinnéide has published them and the portion of the notebook relating to Inishmurray is published in the *Journal of the Galway Archaeological and Historical Society*, 36 (1977-1978), p. 36. From my reading of it and from the lack of other reference to this French consul in native Inishmurray tradition, I do not believe that he actually visited the island but got his information at second hand. See also *Journal of the Galway Archaeological and Historical Society*, 25(1952), p2 and 35(1971), p. 65.

1836. John O'Donovan visited the island for the Ordnance Survey in early July 1836. In this report, which is quoted extensively by Mills in the introduction to Wakeman 1893, he describes the cashel and its buildings as "perhaps the most perfect Cyclopean ruins in the world".

1837. The Roger Chambers Walker's Account Book mentions payment for getting to Inishmurray in August 1837. Petrie was in Rathcarrick from 2 to 25 August; he was ill for the start of his stay and his

work at Carrowmore was done from the 8 to 25 August. Though I can find no Petrie letter or reference to Inishmurray, surely Walker did not go to Inishmurray without Petrie!

1870-?1874. It is not possible to fix an exact date for when Lord Dunraven visited the island but it was sometime between 1870 and 1874. He says "the group of ruins here offers the most characteristic example now in existence of the earliest monastic establishment in Ireland". His five photographs, in his "Notes on Irish Architecture", plates XXV to XXIX inclusive, show the condition of the ruins *before* their "restoration" by the Board of Works in 1880. Some of the photos were subsequently used by Wakeman in his 1893 publication.

1884. The most accurate and detailed account of the island is the 160-page monograph by William F. Wakeman. It is a must for anyone who wishes to acquaint themselves with its history and monastic remains. It was published twice, firstly as "Inis Muiredaich, now Inishmurray, and its Antiquities". *Journal of the Royal Society of Antiquaries of Ireland*, Vol 17 (1885) 175-332, and eight years later as *A Survey of the Antiquarian Remains on the Island of Inishmurray* being the extra volume of the Royal Society of Antiquaries of Ireland for 1892, London 1893. Additional to the original publication there is a twenty-one page preface by James Mills which draws extensively on O'Donovan's 1836 letter, and photographs of the monastic remains of Inishmurray in the 1870s by Dunraven and in 1892 by Robert A.Q. Welch.

During these visits Wakeman made detailed drawings of the monuments and these are bound as *Drawings of the Antiquities on the Island of Inishmurray*, made in the years 1879-1881 for Col. E. Cooper, Markree Castle and are housed in Sligo Library.

Regrettably Wakeman's survey post-dates the "restoration" by the Board of Works in 1880. He frequently derides (19, 25, 28, 54, 74, 103) that work. Wood-Martin in his description of the monastic remains (*History of Sligo*, Vol. 1, 1882, 149-162) is even more scathing, describing the spectacle of "the ghost of the Firbolg architect ... nightly wringing his hands in agony of despair, that nineteenth century gazers should imagine that he was capable of such work". (*History of Sligo*, Vol 1, 1882, 151, fn. 1). Some of the clearance material to the west of the south gate was itself cleared away in recent works.

1892. Robert A.Q. Welch took photographs, some of which were used by Wakeman.

1902. Robert A.Q. Welch was sent to Inishmurray by F.J. Biggar to photograph the monastic sites. He had been on the island in 1892 but that visit was not remembered by the islanders. My mother met him but she did not go to Inishmurray until 1902. He sent my mother a set of Inishmurray photographs and one of the Drumcliffe Cross. I presented those to the Sligo Museum at the time of its establishment in 1954 together with my uncle Patrick's Membership Certificate of the Govan Branch of the Irish National League.

1905. Francis Joseph Biggar, then secretary of the Belfast Naturalists Club, took the photograph of Michael Waters and my father. They had taken him across from Streedagh and encountered fog on the way. He guided them by compass and later presented the compass to my father. It is now in the possession of my sister Mrs Elizabeth Kelly. In the early years of the century, though he never actually met my mother, Biggar corresponded with her requesting specimens and instructing her as to where she might find them.

1934. The notable comment of T.H. Mason was "I shall always remember the dish of lobster, with sauce, which was her [Mrs. Waters, his hostess] speciality. I have eaten lobster in the first class hotels but I have never tasted any so delicious as those on the island of Inishmurray." On Inishmurray lobster was cooked as follows. It was boiled, allowed to cool, then shelled, cut into pieces of about two and a half square centimetres, then fried with a slice of bacon, some butter and some onion, and served hot. I have told this to many people and they, particularly the Cordon Bleu cooks, turned their eyes to heaven. Someone should try it and see if Mason's opinion holds. Incidentally I was in the boat in which Mason returned to the mainland, a passage he graphically describes in his *Islands of Ireland*, 1936.

1935. Winston Churchill came *incognito*. He was a member of a party who came on Lord Londonderry's yacht and was not recognised at the time. Some years afterwards Henry Brady, who was then in England, saw his photograph in a paper and sent the paper to his old pal Jimmy Harte, who was also in England, with the comment "see the little fat man we took around the island the day Lord Londonderry's yacht landed". Jimmy Harte told me afterwards, that Brady and himself spotted this man, who seemed to stay apart from the others, and offered to guide him around the island. He accepted, asking them several questions and made notes "in what did not look like writing", presumably shorthand. In *Teach Molaise*, while making notes, he left his big long cigar down on the altar. To their surprise, Molaise took no umbrage. He gave them five shillings (25p) each, a generous sum in 1935.

1938. Eamon de Valera made a brief visit on the occasion of his maritime tour of the Celtic fringe. He displeased Crimley, i.e., Domnick Harte, by not paying attention to his version of the history of the monastery; this had the consequence of Crimley changing his political allegiance!

1970s. In the early 1970s Charles Conrad, the American astronaut, while a guest of Lord Louis Mountbatten at Mullaghmore, visited the island. I have no record of his impressions of the island but the story is told that on his return he delayed for some time in a hotel in Mullaghmore but, on being pressed to stay longer, declared "Mary – the housekeeper at Classeybawn – will throw me out if I am not back by seven o'clock." It caused much mirth that the local Mary was held in such awe by the man who had journeyed to the moon.

The *Margaret Night* Shipwreck

The *Margaret Night* shipwreck was recorded in *The Sligo Chronicle* for 1 November 1862, as follows:

Shipwreck – Loss of Life on Ennismurray

"On the night of Sunday, 19th October, a vessel, the *Margaret Night* of Blythe, North of England, bound for South America, laden with coals, was blown on the western side of Ennismurray, in Sligo Bay, and in a few hours became a complete wreck. The mate and one seaman were saved but the captain and six of the crew perished. The bodies of the captain and three of the men were washed ashore and buried on the island. The other bodies have not yet been found. The mate and seaman could not leave the island until Wednesday when they landed at Streeda, where they reported themselves to O. Jones, Enq., agent for Lloyds who had every attention paid to the poor fellows. It is pleasing to state that the inhabitants of the island behaved with great kindness to the survivors, supplying them with food and clothing."

The version of Inishmurray people is as follows:

The ship was taking a cargo of potatoes from Sligo to Liverpool. The captain was indisposed and an inexperienced mate was in charge. Before altering course to the North he should have had both Rathlin O'Birne and St. John's Point lighthouses "out", i.e., both lights should be visible from the north of Inishmurray. He changed course with only one light out, that of Rathlin O'Birne and so was wrecked on the western shore of the island.

The names of the survivors were Cooper and Noble; the other names were not recorded locally. Cooper and Noble were saved because they obeyed the age-old advice to stay with the boat. They stayed on the ship which was lying on its side and whose mast was in contact with the shore rock. When daylight came they climbed out along the mast. Cooper taught the islanders how to splice ropes using a marlin spike.

To forestall pilfering from the wreck, Noble coached the man in whose house he stayed to "read" from a salvaged book to the assembled islanders to the effect that pilfering would put the offender at the risk of transportation or even that of hanging. It is said that the book was really a Bible. The "reader's" version was "Anyone interfering with this wreck will be transported or chance to be hung". The joke was that Noble did not know, but the islanders did, that the "reader" was illiterate.

The bodies washed ashore were buried at what has since been known as "The Sailor's Grave". It is just south of the presumed megalithic tomb remains near Classeymore.

The place where the wreck occured is at the west end of the island and has since been known as *Poll an Ancaire* ("the hole of the anchor") as the ships anchor is still there. A second anchor was taken to Streedagh, perhaps as proof of the wreck and lay on the strand there until 1960, when the ex-Inishmurray Waters family moved it to nearby Lucan Point, Streedagh, where it is still.

That the ship was taking potatoes to Liverpool is much more acceptable than that it was in the vicinity of Inishmurray taking coal to South America. There were potatoes washed up on the shore in quantity soon after the wreck.

The obvious error in the newspaper is difficult to understand. I have had several fruitless efforts to find further record of the *Margaret Night*. It is not listed by Lloyds of London. Neither the Irish Maritime Institute in Dún Laoghaire nor John McTernan, Sligo County Librarian and author of *Memory Harbour, The Port of Sligo,* have any record of it. A search for a similar sounding name, the *Margate Knight,* has also proved fruitless.

This was not the first loss of a ship off Inishmurray. In 1739 Rev. William Henry wrote as follows:

"There lies about a league off in the ocean from

Grange a flat island called *Ennismurry* containing about 100 acres [40.47 hectares]. The sea around it is deep but no place for ships or even boats to approach the island with safety. There lies at some distance from the south side a very sharp sunk rock so deep and small in the point as scarce ever to be discovered. This rock about seven years ago proved fatal to a large London galley which in a bright night and perfectly smooth sea, grazed on it with the keel and in a few minutes after sunk to rights, the mariners having barely time to save themselves in the boat. The sea about is very deep.

Natural History and Conservation

Dr Don Cotton, Sligo Regional Technical College

Since the island became uninhabited, the natural history of Inishmurray has substantially altered, the most remarkable change being its colonisation by various sea birds. The breeding colony of storm petrels and the overwintering herd of barnacle geese deserve special mention because they can be classified as of International Importance; and the breeding populations of eider duck and shags are of National Importance. This living, evolving heritage continues to change, and as it does so, some record of the succession is being kept by naturalists. In February 1987 a symposium was held at the Regional Technical College in Sligo entitled "The Future of Inishmurray", and two years later I edited the proceedings which were published as *The Heritage of Inishmurray* (Cotton 1989). As a direct result of the symposium, Inishmurray was placed on a list of Important Bird Areas in Europe (Grimmet & Jones 1989). It was already on the list of Areas of Scientific Interest (ASIs) held by the National Parks and Wildlife Service and was rated as of Regional Importance for ornithological reasons. In 1994 the designation ASI was replaced by that of National Heritage (NHA) with a statutory basis, and Inishmurray is classified as an NHA of Regional Importance.

Geology

It was between 1878 and 1880 that E.T Hardman mapped the rocks of northwest Sligo, including Inishmurray, and since that date there has been no further geological work on the island as far as I can ascertain. He showed that the island is composed of a hard weather resistant sandstone of Lower Carboniferous age (about 330 million years old) with a dip of between 3° and 5° to the southwest. This is the same rock type that forms the cliffs and headlands at Castlegal (extending southwestwards from the mouth of the Duff River) and Mullaghmore Head including Roskeeragh Point below Classie Bawn. It is well known to local fishermen that a reef continues out under the sea from Roskeeragh Point towards

Inishmurray, and to a geologist this is confirmation that the island is just an extension of this same highly resistant bed of rock. It is believed that these rocks were deposited in the delta a large river flowing from a continent to the north and into a sea to the south because there are ripple marks, cross-bedding and occasional fossils that all indicate such conditions and include evidence of the direction of water flow.

The only other geological deposits on Inishmurray are of a much more recent origin as they only date back to the last glaciation (the Midlandian of between 75,000 and 10,000 years ago) of the Pleistocene "ice ages". These loose deposits of crushed rocks and clays form an irregular blanket over most of the eastern end of the island. The poor drainage caused by these deposits influenced the soils and agriculture and in places peats developed which were mostly cut away again by the inhabitants in recent times. A combination of old sandstone rocks that produce only the thinnest of soils, impervious glacial deposits that hamper drainage, and exposure to the Atlantic gales, must have made it almost impossible to grow a decent crop on the island and contributed considerably to the hardship of life in such a remote place.

Plants Recorded from Inishmurray

Several botanists have made lists of the flora of Inishmurray, but none of these studies would claim to have been fully comprehensive. The first list was made by Praeger and Barrington during a one hour visit on 8 June 1896. They recorded 145 species of flowering plants and ferns and many years later Praeger concluded that Inishmurray "offers no special attraction to the botanist" (Praeger 1934). The complete list of species recorded by Praeger and Barrington appears to be lost to science but the more important finds are described in Prager (1896). A second list of the flora was made by Drs Micheline Sheehy Skeffington and Peter Wyse Jackson during a one day trip by Dublin Naturalists' Field Club in

1980 which was published in Cotton (*op.cit.*) as was a list of 124 species compiled by Bob Davidson when he stayed on the island for several days in 1981. Since that date, observations on the flora have been made by Joan Carson, Jim Fitzharris and myself, Don Cotton. The following list is a compilation of all the knowledge just described and broadly follows that published in Cotton (*op.cit.*) but with minor modifications and corrections.

Ferns

Anthyrium filix-femina (lady-fern)

Asplenium marinum (sea spleenwort)

Blechnum spicant (hard fern)

Dryopteris dilatata (broad buckler-fern)

Dryopteris filix-mas (male fern)

Ophioglossum vulgatum
(adder's-tongue)

Osmunda regalis (royal fern)

Polypodium vulgare (polypody)

Pteridium aquilinum (bracken)

Flowering plants

Achillea millefolium (milfoil or yarrow)

Agrimonia eupatoria (agrimony)

Agrostis stolonifera (creeping bent)

Aira praecox (early hair-grass)

Allium babingtonii (Babington's leek)

Alopecurus geniculatus (marsh foxtail)

Anacamptis pyramidalis
(pyramidal orchid)

Anagallis arvensis (scarlet pimpernel)

Anagallis tenella (bog pimpernel)

Angelica sylvestris (wild angelica)

Anthoxanthum odoratum
(sweet vernal-gr.)

Anthyllis vulneraria (kidney vetch)

Apium graveolens (wild celery)

Apium inundatum (lesser marshwort)

Apium nodiflorum (fool's watercress)

Arctium lappa (greater burdock)

Arctium minus agg. (burdock)

Armeria maritima (sea pink or thrift)

Arrhenatherum elatius (false oat)

Atriplex sp. (orache)

Bellis perennis (daisy)

Brassica sp.

Bromus hordeaceus (soft-brome)

Calluna vulgaris (heather or ling)

Caltha palustris (marsh marigold)

Capsella bursa-pastoris
(shepherd's purse)

Cardamine pratensis (cuckoo flower)

Carex demissa (common yellow-sedge)

Carex distans (distant sedge)

Carex echinata (star sedge)

Carex flacca (glaucous sedge)

Carex nigra (common sedge)

Carex panicea (carnation sedge)

Centaurea nigra (common knapweed)

Centaurium erythraea
(common centaury)

Cerastium fontanum (common mouse-ear)

Chamomilla sauveolens (pineapple weed)

Cirsium dissectum (meadow thistle)

Cirsium arvense (creeping thistle)

Cirsium palustre (marsh thistle)

Cirsium vulgare (spear thistle)

Cochlearia officinalis (scurvy grass)

Cochlearia scotica
(Scottish scurvy grass)

Cynosurus cristatus (crested dog's-tail)

Dactylis glomerata (cock's-foot grass)

Dactylorhiza fuchsii
(common spotted-orchid)

Dactylorhiza maculata
(heath spotted-orch.)

Digitalis purpurea (foxglove)

Drosera rotundifolia
(round-leaved sundew)

Eleocharis palustris
(common spike-rush)

Empetrum nigrum (crowberry)

Erica cinerea (bell heather)

Erica tetralix (cross-leaved heath)

Eriophorum angustifolium (bog cotton)

Eriophorum vaginatum
(hare's-tail cottongr.)

Euphrasia sp. (eyebright)

Festuca ovina (sheep's fescue)

Festuca rubra (red fescue)

Filipendula ulmaria (meadowsweet)

Galium aparine (cleavers)

Galium palustre
(common marsh-bedstraw)

Galium saxatile (heath bedstraw)

Geranium dissectum (cut-leaved cranesbill)

Geranium molle (soft cranesbill)

Geranium robertianum (herb-Robert)

Geum rivale (water avens)

Glyceria fluitans (floating sweet-grass)

Gnaphalium uliginosum (marsh cudweed)

Hedera helix (ivy)

Heracleum sphondylium (hogweed)

Hippuris vulgaris (mare's-tail)

Holcus lanatus (Yorkshire fog)

Hyacinthoides non-scripta (bluebell)

Hydrocotyle vulgaris (marsh pennywort)

Hypochoeris radicata (cat's-ear)

Iris pseudacorus (yellow flag iris)

Juncus articulatus (jointed rush)

Juncus bufonius (toad rush)

Juncus conglomeratus (compact rush)

Juncus effusus (soft rush)

Juncus inflexus (hard rush)

Juncus squarrosus (heath rush)

Lamium purpureum (red dead-nettle)

Lemna minor (common duckweed)

Leontodon hispidus (rough hawkbit)

Leucanthemum vulgare (oxeye daisy)

Listera ovata (common twayblade)

Lolium perenne (perennial rye-grass)

Lonicera periclymenum (honeysuckle)

Lotus corniculatus (bird's foot trefoil)

Luzula campestris (field wood-rush)

Luzula multiflora (heath wood-rush)

Lychnis flos-cuculi (ragged robin)

Lythrum portula (water purslane)

Lythrum salicaria (purple loosestrife)

Matricaria maritima (sea mayweed)

Menyanthes trifoliata (bog bean)

Molinia caerulea (purple moor-grass)

Myosotis arvensis (field forget-me-not)

Myosotis discolor (changing forget-me-not)

Myosotis laxa (tufted forget-me-not)

Myosotis scorpioides (water forget-me-not)

Nardus stricta (mat-grass)

Narthecium ossifragum (bog asphodel)

Odonites verna (red bartsia)

Oenanthe crocata
   (hemlock water dropwort)

Pedicularis palustris (marsh lousewort)

Pedicularis sylvatica (lousewort)

Petasites hybridus (butterbur)

Phragmites australis (common reed)

Plantago coronopus (buck's-horn plantain)

Plantago lanceolata (ribwort plantain)

Plantago major (great plantain)

Plantago maritima (sea plantain)

Platanthera bifolia
   (lesser butterfly-orchid)

Platanthera chlorantha
   (gr. butterfly orchid)

Poa trivialis (rough meadow-grass)

Polygala vulgaris (common milkwort)

Polygonum persicaria (redshank)

Potamogeton natans (broad-lvd pondweed)

Potamogeton polygonifolius
   (bog pondweed)

Potentilla anserina (silverweed)

Potentilla erecta (tormentil)

Potentilla palustris (marsh cinquefoil)

Potentilla reptans (creeping cinqufoil)

Prunella vulgaris (selfheal)

Radiola linoides (allseed)

Ranunculus acris (meadow buttercup)

Ranunclus flammula (lesser spearwort)

Ranunculus repens (creeping buttercup)

Rubus fruticosus agg. (bramble)

Rumex acetosella (sheep's sorrel)

Rumex acetosa (common sorrel)

Rumex crispus (curled dock)

Rumex hibernicus (Irish sorrel)

Rumex obtusifolius (broad-leaved duck)

Sagina maritima (sea pearlwort)

Salix cinerea oleifolia (rusty willow)

Salix repens (creeping willow)

Scirpus fluitans (floating club-rush)

Sedum album (white stonecrop)

Sedum anglicum (English stonecrop)

Senecio aquaticus (marsh ragwort)

Senecio jacobaea (common ragwort)

Senecio vulgaris (groundsel)

Silene dioica (red campion)

Silene vulgaris maritima (sea campion)

Sinapis alba (white mustard)

Solidago virgaurea (goldenrod)

Sonchus asper (prickly sow-thistle)

Sonchus oleraceus (smooth sow-thistle)

Sparganium erectum (branched bur-reed)

Spergularia media (greater sea-spurry)

Spergularia rupicola (rock sea-spurry)

Stachys palustris (marsh woundwort)

Stellaria alsine (bog stitchwort)

Stellaria media (common chickweed)

Succisa pratensis (devil's-bit scabious)

Symphytum sp. (comfrey)

Taraxacum officinale agg. (dandelion)

Trifolium repens (white clover)

Trifolium pratense (red clover)

Triglochin palustris (marsh arrowgrass)

Umbilicus rupestris (wall pennywort)

Urtica dioica (stinging nettle)

Veronica chamaedrys

   (germander speedwell)

Veronica persica

   (common field-speedwell)

Vicia cracca (tufted vetch)

Vicia sepium (bush vetch)

Viola riviniana (common dog-violet)

The foregoing list of plants contains 179 species and is certainly not yet complete, but with the following few notes, it gives a good indication of what the island has to offer by way of habitats for the fauna. Much of the island is covered in a low-growing maritime grassland, and like many other uninhabited offshore islands, flowers such as the bluebell, sea pink and scurvy grass are in abundance and provide a memorable experience for those who visit in May. In recent years the bracken and brambles have shown their considerable ability to spread and form dense cover at the expense of the other plant species. This is good news for the eider duck which use such cover to hide their nests. At the same time, the marsh behind the cashel has become more extensive as the outlet has become blocked and this has allowed the associated flora to spread to new areas. The above list contains many wetland species with plants such as the common reed and yellow flag iris being obvious, but less common species like the marsh cudweed, lesser marshwort and branched bur-reed are also present. The herb-rich marshes are important places for damselflies and other insects as well as providing habitat for snipe, duck and sedge warblers.

There are no real rarities amongst the plants of the island, but a few species that are not generally common on the mainland can be briefly mentioned. Of the ferns, the adder's-tongue can be a difficult species to find but is known from a number of coastal sites in Sligo and on Inishmurray can be seen at the extreme eastern tip beside the path. The royal fern is also a local species on the mainland and on Inishmurray. It is in the marsh behind the cashel. Allseed is a weed of agriculture that is now scarce in Ireland but survives along an old track leading in to the marsh from the west. One of the most interesting species is the Babington's leek which is very local in distribution in Ireland and which often grows where monastic sites were located. Its presence on Inishmurray therefore compounds this view. Finally, the Scottish scurvy grass and the Irish sorrel are interesting species which have a limited Irish distribution and have been recorded on the island by Peter Wyse Jackson and Michelle Sheehy Skeffington.

An Annotated List of the Animals Recorded on Inishmurray

The only aspect of the fauna which has received any serious attention is the bird life. The first serious attempt to record the birds was by I.K. Gibson, J.P. Hillis, C.F. McLoughlin and R.F. Ruttledge who published their observations in the *Irish Bird Report* for 1955 as well as in a paper by Ruttledge (1956). In 1961 David Cabot spent almost five days on the island and published his results (Cabot 1962) and the ringing studies of Joan Carson from 1977 to 1986 were summarised in Cotton (1989). All bird data refer to summering birds as no ornithologist has visited the island at other times since it became uninhabited. Invertebrate data is mainly from my own observations.

Beetles

   Carabus problematicus (ground beetle)

Bivalves shells

   Mytilus edulis (Common mussel

Butterflies and moths

   Clouded yellow (*Colias croceus*)

   Common blue (*Polyommatus icarus*)

   Forester moth (*Adscita statices*)

   Green-veined white (*Pieris napae*)

   Large white (*Pieris brassicae*)

   Meadow brown (*Maniola jurtina*)

Painted lady (*Cynthia cardui*)

Red admiral (*Vanessa atalanta*)

Small heath (*Coenonympha pamphilus*)

Small tortoiseshell *(Aglais urticae)*

Small white (*Pieris rapae*)

Wall (*Lasiommata megera*)

Speckled wood (*Pararge aegeria*)

Dragonflies and damselflies

Coenagrion pulchellum

Enallagma cyathigerum (common blue)

Ischnura elegans (blue-tailed damsel)

Pyrrhosoma nymphula (red damselfly)

Earthworms

Aporrectodea caliginosa

Lumbricus festivus

Earwigs

Fortficula auricularia (common earwig)

Millipedes

Cylindriolus latestriatus

Brachydesmus superus

Sea Anemones

Actinea aquina

Snails

Cepaea nemoralis

Discus rotundatus

Gibbula cineraria

Limax maximus (great gey slug)

Nassarias incrassatus

Patella vulgata (common limpet)

Vallonia pulchella

Three--pronged bristletails

Petrobius sp.

True flies

Episyrphus balteatus (hoverfly)

Eristalinus aeneus (hoverfly)

Eristalinus sepulchralis (hoverfly)

Haematopota pluvialis (horsefly-cleg)

Platycheirus immarginatus (hoverfly)

Pyrophaena granditarsa (hoverfly)

Woodlice

Ligia oceanica (sea slater)

Oniscus asellus

Philoscia muscorum

Porcellio scaber

Birds

Blackbird (*Turdus merula*) Probably two or three pairs breed in most years.

Bunting, reed (*Emberiza schoeniclus*) Thought to be probably breeding in the 1970s but not seen on the island in recent years.

Bunting, snow (*Plectrophenax nivalis*) One on 20 May 1978 was seen by David Scott and Noel Murphy.

Cormorant (*Phalacorcorax carbo*) Occasionally seen on the island but has never been known to breed.

Corncrake (*Crex crex*) Used to be present in large numbers pre-1948 (Heraughty in this volume). There were two pairs in 1961 (Cabot 1962) and the species was heard calling in 1969 (Merne pers.comm.) but there is no evidence of its present on the island since then.

Crow, hooded (*Corvus corone cornix*) Have bred on the island in the 1970s but recent sightings are of non-breeders.

Curlew (*Numenius arquata*) Occasionally noted in the summer but not breeding.

Dove, collared (*Streptopelia decaocto*) One was seen on the island in 1992.

Dove, rock (*Columba livia*) A pair is often seen on the island and once confirmed as breeding.

Dunlin (*Calidris alpina*) Occasional summer occurrences probably indicate spasmodic breeding. Joan Carson saw an immature one on the island in 1990.

Dunnock (*Prunella modularis*) Several birds, which presumably breed.

Eider (*Somateria mollissima*) The eider duck only first bred in Ireland in 1912 but it was not until July 1961 that up to 56 were counted which included very young chicks giving very strong circumstantial evidence of breeding for the first time (Cabot 1962). Since then the breeding population has been well established with about 100 breeding pairs being suspected from counts of males around the island in the breeding season.

Falcon, peregrine (*Falco peregrinus*) One found shot on 20 May 1978.

Fulmar (*Fulmarus glacialis*) First recorded as breeding in 1979 by Joan Carson who saw three pairs. Since then the number of breeding birds had increased to 28 pairs in 1992.

Gannet (*Sula Bassana*) Regularly seen offshore but do not set foot on the island.

Godwit, bar-tailed (*Limosa lapponica*) Present in 1986 and 1990, but not breeding.

Goose, barnacle (*Branta Leucopsis*) The flock of barnacle geese associated with Lissadell and various other mainland locations along the north coast of Sligo use Inishmurray as an autumn feeding site and as a safe roosting site throughout the winter. If it is assumed that counts made on the mainland reflect the number of birds using the island then in the early 1980s there were 500 geese and in the early 1990s the flock had grown dramatically to 2000 geese. It should be noted that the size of this flock has been of International Importance for at least 10 years.

Goose, white-fronted (*Anser albifrons*) There is no proof of birds actually over-wintering on the island but they have been seen flying high to and from that direction by several observers.

Greenshank (*Tringa nebularia*) One recorded in 1970 by Oscar Merne.

Guillemot (*Urla aalge*) Occasionally seen offshore but not breeding.

Guillemot, black (*Cepphus grylle*) It is believed that between 5 and 10 pairs bred every year.

Gull, black-headed (*Larus ridibundus*) Often present in small numbers and occasionally a few pairs breed.

Gull, common *(Larus canus)* Often present in small numbers and usually a few pairs (less than 10) breed.

Gull, great black-backed (*Larus marinus*) Up to 40 pairs bred here during the 1960s, then in the 1970s numbers rose to over 200 pairs. Botulism effected this species in the 1980s and numbers fell to around 80 pairs.

Gull, herring (*Larus argentatus*) This species was present but not breeding in 1955 but by 1961 there were 150 breeding pairs. The colony continued to gain strength with 310

pairs in 1970/71 and an estimated 880 pairs in 1979. In the early 1980s outbreaks of botulism began to take an annual toll and the colony now fluctuates between 150 and 400 pairs. A pullus (nestling) rung here on 26 June 1979 was found dead at Cleveley's Blackpool, England on 29 September 1979.

Gull, lesser black-backed (*Larus fuscus*) Was not breeding up to 1961 but by 1976 was confirmed as a breeding species. By the mid-1980s there were 30 breeding pairs and the colony continues to gain strength into the 1990s.

Greenshank (*Tringa nebularia*) One recorded in 1970 by Oscar Merne.

Heron, grey (*Ardea cinerea*) One recorded in 1979 and again in 1990.

Kittiwake (*Rissa tridactyla*) Often seen flying offshore but does not breed on the island, probably due to the lack of suitable cliffs.

Lapwing (*Vanellus vanellus*) Two or three pairs are usually present in the breeding season but only breeds occasionally.

Linnet (*Acanthis cannabina*) Noted in 1986 and 1990 by Joan Carson.

Mallard (*Anas platyrhynchos*) Probably breed every years with up to 10 pairs confirmed as breeding in 1986.

Moorhen (*Gallinula chloropus*) One pair in 1961 (Cabot 1962).

Oystercatcher (*Haematopus ostralegus*) Breeds, with up to 20 pairs in some years. Large flock of 300 were noted as roosting on the island in August 1986.

Petrel, Leach's storm (*Oceanodroma leucorhoa*) One was seen over the sea between Inishmurray and Mullaghmore on 10 July 1977 by D. Scott and N. Murphy.

Petrel, storm *(Hydrobates pelagicus)* Heraughty has indicated that the species probably bred when he lived on the island in the late 1940s when birds nesting in a particular "fence" were called *cloclánn* by the islanders. However, it was not until 1977 that they were "scientifically" proven to breed in the same stone wall and it was considered likely that the colony was well established at that time. In 1981 the colony had spread to holes in walls not previously occupied. The size of the colony is not precisely known but in 1979 it was estimated that there were 500 pairs. A ringing programme by Joan Carson has demonstrated a great deal of interaction between the Inishmurray birds and those of other similar islands including Inishglora, The Mullet, county Mayo; Rathlin O'Birne, Inishduff and Roaninish, county Donegal; Copeland, county Down; Ailsa Craig, St. Kilda, Thurso Sanda Island and Noss Head in Scotland; and Calf of Man, England. An interesting recovery of a storm petrel ringed at Inishmurray on 21 August 1984 was found dead at Nilonyana, Transkai, South Africa just four months later on 27 December 1984.

Phalarope, red-necked (*Phalaropus lobatus*) Unsubstantiated rumours of this species being present in the 1970s which is interesting because it occasionally breeds in Ireland in similar places.

Pigeon, wood (*Columba palumbus*) Breeding was suspected in the 1970s but not seen on the island in recent years.

Pipit, meadow (*Anthus pratensis*) About two pairs breed on the island in most years.

Pipit, rock (*Anthus spinoletta*) About 10 pairs breed on the island.

Plover, ringed (*Charadrius hiaticula*) A few pairs probably breed every year.

Puffin (*Fratercula arctica*) Occasionally seen offshore but not breeding.

Raven (*Corvus corax*) One pair bred in 1961 (Cabot 1962) but recent sightings are probably of non-breeders.

Razorbill (*Alca torda*) Occasionally seen offshore but not breeding.

Redshank (*Tringa totantis*) Up to 10 in July 1961 but not noted in recent years. Could potentially breed here.

Robin (*Erithacus rubecula*) One pair breeds in most years.

Sandpiper, purple (*Calidris maritima)* One on 18 July 1961 (Cabot 1962); and more than 27 on 18 May 1985 (D.Cotton) which are interesting occurrences for a bird that is regarded as a winter visitor to Ireland.

Scoter, common (*Melanitta nigra*) Sixty seen off the end of the island on 18-20 August 1986.

Shag (*Phalacrocorax aristotelis*) In 1955 there was only one shag noted on the island, in 1961 there were up to 22 shags and they were probably breeding but it was not until 1969 that they were proven to breed. Throughout the 1980s and into the 1990s the breeding population has risen to Nationally Important levels with over 300 pairs in some years but 150 pairs in others. Ringed birds are mostly recovered locally from Mayo, Sligo and Leitrim, but a shag ringed at Inishmurray on 2 June 1985 was found dead at Mull, Strathclyde, Scotland on 30 May 1987.

Shank, red (*Tringa totanus*) Up to 10 in July 1961 but not noted in recent years. Could potentially breed here.

Shearwater, Manx (*Puffinus puffinus*) Frequently seen out to sea but doesn't appear to land or breed on the island.

Shelduck (*Tadorna tadorna*) Noted several times, and one pair bred in 1992.

Shoveler (*Anas clypeata*) One male present on 18 May 1985.

Skua, arctic (*Stercorarius parasiticus*) Sometimes one is seen following the boat over to the island in early summer.

Skylark (*Alanda arvensis*) Bred here in the 1970s but only occasionally seen here in recent years.

Snipe (*Gallinago gallinago*) Small numbers breed every year.

Sparrow, house or tree? (*Passer domesticus/montanus*) Noted by Heraughty when the island was inhabited, but no sightings since then.

Starling (*Sturnus vulgaris*) Often present and possibly breeding.

Swallow (*Hirundo rustica)* A pair breeds on the island in most years.

Swift (*Apus apus*) Used to be present in large numbers (Heraughty) but not seen over the last number of years.

Teal (*Anas crecca*) A few are usually present in the breeding season and one and two pairs were confirmed as breeding in 1981 and 1986 respectively.

Tern, arctic (*Sterna paradisea*) A hitherto unrecorded colony of 500-1000 birds was found here in 1955 (Ruttledge 1956); there were 400-450 pairs in 1961 (Cabot 1962) making this the largest colony in Ireland at the time. Since then the species has been very up and down with none in 1970/71; 50 pairs were estimated in 1977, 250 pairs in 1979, 154 pairs in 1981, only one in 1983, 5 pairs in 1984, 4 pairs in 1985, 60 pairs in 1986, and 40 pairs in 1992. Heraughty has told me that terns, locally called *gúróg*, were breeding on Inishmurray in the 1940s, although the species involved was not known to him.

Tern, black (*Chlidonias niger*) One present in June/July 1981 was recorded by Joan Carson.

Tern, common (*Sterna hirundo*) A large colony was discovered here in 1955 (Ruttledge 1956) which comprised of 100-150 pairs in 1961 (Cabot 1962) but there were none in 1970/71 (O.Meirne). Two were present in 1981.

Tern, little (*Sterna albifrons*) About 10 pairs evidently breeding in 1955 (Ruttledge 1956); 1 pair not proven to be breeding in 1961 (Cabot 1962) and not seen on the island since.

Tern, sandwich (*Sterna sandvicensis*) One pair bred in 1981 but often not present in the breeding season at all.

Tern, roseate (*Sterna dougallii*) A pair bred in 1955 (Ruttledge 1956) and a pair was present in 1961 but not proven to breed (Cabot 1962).

Thrush, song (*Turdus philomelos*) One or two pairs probably breed in most years.

Turnstone (*Arenaria interpres*) A few are present most summers but they do not breed in Ireland.

Warbler, grasshopper (*Locustella naevia*) A pair probably breed in most years.

Warbler, sedge (*Acrocephalus schoenabaenus*) Probably one or two pairs breed in most years.

Wheatear (*Oenanthe oenanthe*) Probably two or three pairs breed in most years.

Whimbrel (*Numenius phaeopus*) One seen on the island by Joan Carson in 1986.

Whitethroat (*Sylvia communis*) Two or three breeding pairs in 1961 (Cabot 1962).

Wren (*Troglodytes troglodytes*) The number of breeding pairs appears to have dwindled from an estimated 25 in 1961 (Cabot 1962) to about 10 pairs in recent years.

Mammals (Chordata ; Vertebrata; Mammalia)

Mice (*Mus/Apodemus*) Heraughty has described both grey mice and brown mice as being on the island which would suggest that both the house mouse and field mouse were present.

Rabbit (*Oryctolagus cuniculus*) Small population noted on the island in 1981.

Seal, grey (*Halichoerus grypus*) Heraughty notes that there was a "colony" of grey seals on the Bomore Rocks to the north of the island. It is likely that they breed on the island in the winter months. Often seen just off the island.

References

Cabot, D.B. (1962) "An ornithological expedition to Inishmurray, Co. Sligo", *Irish Naturalists' Journal* 14(3):59-61. (Corrigendum on page 128).

Cotton, D.C.F. (1989)(ed.) *The Heritage of Inishmurray*. Regional Technical College, Sligo. 103 pages.

Grimmett, R.F.A. & T.A. JONES (1989) *Important Bird Areas in Europe*. ICBP Technical Publication No.9. International Council for Bird Preservation/International Waterfowl and Wetlands Research Bureau, Cambridge.

Praeger, R.L. (1896) "The plants of Inishmurray, Co. Sligo", Irish Naturalist 5:177-178.

Praeger, R.L., *The Botanist in Ireland*, 1954: Hodges, Figgis & Co., Dublin.

Ruttledge, R.F., "An ornithological visit to Inishmurray", *Irish Naturalists' Journal* 12:28-29, 1956.

APPENDIX 6

The People of the Island

At the prompting of Martin A. Timoney, inspired by the work on another Atlantic island by Allan Crawford, Tristan da Cunha and the *Roaring Forties*, Cape Town 1982, particularly pp. 90-91, I have collected and arranged the names and years of birth of people living on Inishmurray since 1802. My sources were the school roll books, personal memory and the Ahamlish parish registers. In some cases all I know is that there were so many children in a particular house.

Comparative facts on these two far apart Atlantic islands are as follows. Inishmurray has certainly been inhabited since early Christian times, if not from the Iron Age or even the Bronze Age; Tristan da Cunha was first discovered in 1506 by Tristao d'Achuna from Portugal, but the modern foundations were in 1802 and 1816. Only 25.50 hectares (63 acres) of the 90.25 hectares (223 acres) of Inishmurray, which rises to no more than 23.54 metres (77 feet) above sea level, are good arable land; the rest is shallow peat. Only 5.18 sq km (2 sq miles) of the 87.42 sq km (38 sq miles) of Tristan are usable as its volcanic peak rises 2,035.76 metres (6,679 feet) above the Southern Atlantic. Inishmurray is 7.26 km (4.5 miles) from the nearest mainland while Tristan is all of 2,413.50 km (1,500 miles) from southern Africa, making it the farthest away inhabited place from other inhabited land in the world. Both had a very limited number of family surnames. Counting those present for two generations at least Inishmurray had Heraughty, Brady, Waters, Harte, Hoey, Donlon, Mannion, McGowan and Boyle; for Tristan they are Hagan, Rogers, Glass, Lavarello, Swain, Green and Repetto. At the time of abandonment in 1948 there were only 46 people living on Inishmurray, though the maximum at any one time seems to have been in the 1890s when it was 102 and there we have record of 257 people being born to those

living on the island. Inishmurray was abandoned in 1948; the current population of Tristan is under 300. Both islands were very dependent on fish. Poteen in the case of Inishmurray and crayfish in the case of Tristan were the main sources of income.

What follows is (1) the sequence of heads of households and (2) a full list of those born to people living on the island since Domhnall Heraughty settled on Inishmurray in 1802. Domhnall's father was Tadhg of Ballyconnell who had lived there in the 1760s. Counting from Tadhg to my grandchildren there have been eight generations.

The houses (marked A to O) in the following table are shown on the map on pXXX. The house in which Domhnall Heraughty and his son Patrick or Pádraig lived subsequently became the R.I.C. Barracks. It was later used as a byre/barn by the Waters family. It was situated about 90 metres (100yds) SW of the cashel facing SW. Access to the north of the island was by a lane from the present road and ran in a NW direction. When the house became the R.I.C. barracks my grandfather, Martin, had taken over the first school, House A, and converted it into a dwelling house. The new school had just been built as an addition to House B (Waters) on the east end of that house about 1866. The latest school was built in 1899 as a replacement for this. His half-brother, Michael Waters, had built another house, House B (Waters), on the present road.

There was a house belonging to Micky Beag Dunleavy about 27 metres (30 yds) northwest of Ollamurray on the west side of the lane leading to the commonage on the north of the island. This lane with the lane on the east of the island leading from either end of the main road to the commonage were famine relief works and both have kerbs which the road does not have. The western lane was dubbed "Stirabout Lane" as the daily wage was a portion of Indian meal.

Heads of Houses

The heads of houses, lettered from west to east (see map on p. 76), were as set out below. Houses F, G, K and M were originally Heraughty property.

1802 Settlers	Holdings by 1890	Houses from W-E	Houses at 1802	Second Generation	Third Generation	Fourth Generation	Fifth Generation
DH¹	Heraughty	A²	Domhnall	Pádraig s. Domhnall first "King"	Martin d.1890s half-br. Michael W.	Martin b. 1868 d. 1917	Patrick b.1912 (Sligo)
	Waters	B		Michael	Michael half-br. Martin H. b. 1841	John last "King" b. 1879	b. 1914 (Moneygold)
	Harte	C		Harry m.d. James	Domhnall b. 1866	Dominick b. 1936	Dominick b. 1936
DH¹	Heraughty	D	O'Leary	James s. Domhnall	John	Martin b.1890 d. 1922	John Francis b. 1912 d. Sooey
	Heraughty	E	Meehan		Dan d.. 1918	Dan b.1892 d. 1940s in Lisslarry left I. 1924	Patrick Joseph b. 1926 I. Lisslarry
DH¹	Boyle	F		Michael Boyle m.d. Domhnall from Sooey	John did not marry d. Sooey		
DH¹	McGowan	G		Michael McGowan m.d. Domhnall	Michael 1849-1930 did not marry		
SB³	Brady	H		Harry s. Sean	Henry b. 1889	Patrick b. 1917	Patrick Joseph
SB³	Brady	I	Brady	John s. Seán	John	"Red" Michael	John b. 1928
SB³	Brady	J	Brady		Páid and Seán	Michael	Patrick
DH¹	Hoey	K		Michael Hoey m.d. Domhnall	James Donlon m. Cathy Hoey d. Ml. Hoey	Joseph b. 1902	Patrick b. 1939
DH¹	Heraughty	L	Currid	Michael s. Domhnall	Michael "Ruadh" b.1859	Dan b.1879	
DH¹	Mannion	M			John Mannion m. Bridget H.	James	(USA)
	Donleavy	O			hired hand to Martin Heraughty d.1920s		

1. DH = descendant of Domhnall Heraughty

2. Actually later barracks

3. SB = descendant of Sean Brady

People Born to those Born on Inishmurray

Christian Name	Surname	Born	House	Notes
?	HERAUGHTY		A	
?	HERAUGHTY		A	
?	HERAUGHTY		A	
PATRICK	HERAUGHTY		A	of Domhnall,b. ?1803-1820
JAMES	HERAUGHTY		A	of Domhnall,b.?1803-1820
MICHAEL	HERAUGHTY		A	of Domhnall,b.?1803-1820
BRIDGET	HERAUGHTY		A	of Domhnall,b.?1803-1820
KATHLEEN	HERAUGHTY		A	of Domhnall,b.?1803-1820
MARY	HERAUGHTY		A	of Domhnall,b.?1803-1820
? daughter	HERAUGHTY		A	of Domhnall,b.?1803-1820
? daughter	HERAUGHTY		A	of Domhnall,b.?1803-1820
? son	HERAUGHTY		A	of Domhnall,b.?1803-1820
MARTIN	HERAUGHTY		A	b. 1830s, drowned 1880s
MARTIN	HERAUGHTY	1868	A	
PATRICK	HERAUGHTY	1870	A	
JOHN	HERAUGHTY	1871	A	
BRIDGET	HERAUGHTY	1874	A	**
BRIDGET	HERAUGHTY	1882	A	
JOHN	HERAUGHTY	1883	A	
MARTIN	HERAUGHTY	1888	A	
MARGARET	HERAUGHTY	1894	A	
MARY ANN	HERAUGHTY	1895	A	
MARY	HERAUGHTY	1908	A	l. Cliffoney, Sligo
CHRISTINA	HERAUGHTY	1909	A	l. Blackpool; Mrs Barry
MARTHA	HERAUGHTY	1910	A	d. 1972
PATRICK	HERAUGHTY	1912	A	l. Sligo; author
ELIZABETH	HERAUGHTY	1914	A	l. Sligo; Mrs Kelly
MARTIN	HERAUGHTY	1917	A	d. 1993
? daughter	WATERS		B	
? daughter	WATERS		B	
? daughter	WATERS		B	
? daughter	WATERS		B	
? daughter	WATERS		B	
? daughter	WATERS		B	
? daughter	WATERS		B	
? daughter	WATERS		B	
? daughter	WATERS		B	
ANN	WATERS		B	m. Harry Brady of Ho H
MICHAEL	WATERS	1841	B	3rd "King" of Inishmurray
ANN NORA	WATERS	1871	B	**
ANN	WATERS	1875	B	**
SARA JANE	WATERS	1876	B	**
MICHAEL	WATERS	1876	B	Last "King" m. MaryAnn Mannion Ho M z.

Christian Name	Surname	Born	House	Notes	
MARY	WATERS	1880	B		
KATE	WATERS	1882	B		
JOHN ANDREW	WATERS	1886	B		
JAMES	WATERS	1888	B	**	
JOHN ANDREW	WATERS	1914	B		
MICHAEL	WATERS	1915	B		
MARY	WATERS	1917	B		
SARAH	WATERS	1919	B	l. Blackrock, Dublin	
PATRICK	WATERS	1921	B		
? daughter	HARTE		C		
? daughter	HARTE		C		
? daughter	HARTE		C		
ANN	HARTE		C	m. in Cloonagh	
JAMES	HARTE	1856	C		
JOHN	HARTE	1858	C		
DOMINICK	HARTE	1866	C	z	
HENRY	HARTE	1868	C		
CATHERINE	HARTE	1870	C	**	
NORA	HARTE	1876	C	**	
MARY ANN	HARTE	1903	C		
JOHN	HARTE	1905	C		
DOMNICK	HARTE	1907	C	m. Jane Heraughty of Ho L	z.
FLORENCE	HARTE	1913	C	l. Lisslary Grange; Mrs Brady	
JAMES	HARTE	1916	C		
CHRISTY	HARTE	1933	C	l. Luton	z.
MARY	HARTE	1934	C	l. Luton	z.
PEGGY	HARTE	1935	C	l. Luton	z.
DOMINICK	HARTE	1936	C	l. London	z.
PATRICK	HARTE	1939	C	l. London	z.
?	HERAUGHTY		D		
?	HERAUGHTY		D		
?	HERAUGHTY		D		
DAN	HERAUGHTY		D		
JOHN	HERAUGHTY		D		
PEGGY	HERAUGHTY		D		
MARY	HERAUGHTY	1870	D	**	
FRANCIS	HERAUGHTY	1872	D	**	
BRIDGET	HERAUGHTY	1874	D	**	
NORA	HERAUGHTY	1878	D	**	
JAMES	HERAUGHTY	1879	D	**	
KATE	HERAUGHTY	1888	D		
CATHERINE	HERAUGHTY	1889	D	**	
DAN	HERAUGHTY	1890	D	Twin of Martin	
MARTIN	HERAUGHTY	1890	D	Twin of Dan	
PATRICK	HERAUGHTY	1892	D		

Christian Name	Surname	Born	House	Notes
JOHN FRANCIS	HERAUGHTY	1912	D	m. Kathleen Brady of Ho J
?	HERAUGHTY		E	
BRIDGET	HERAUGHTY	1866	E	**
JOHN	HERAUGHTY	1869	E	
PATRICK	HERAUGHTY	1871	E	
MARTIN	HERAUGHTY	1872	E	**
FRANCIS	HERAUGHTY	1881	E	**
PATRICK	HERAUGHTY	1882	E	**
MICHAEL	HERAUGHTY	1884	E	
CATHERINE	HERAUGHTY	1887	E	**
DAN	HERAUGHTY	1892	E	
NORA	HERAUGHTY	1903	E	
? son	HERAUGHTY	1920	E	d. early 1920s
MARY KATE	HERAUGHTY	1921	E	l. England
BRIDGET	HERAUGHTY	1924	E	l. Inishcrone
PATRICK JOSEPH	HERAUGHTY	1926	E	l. England
NORA ELLEN	HERAUGHTY	1928	E	l. Athlone
DAN	HERAUGHTY	1931	E	l. England
JAMES CHRISTOPHER	HERAUGHTY	1933	E	l. Moneygold
?	SCANLON		F	
?	SCANLON		F	
?	SCANLON		F	
JOHN	BOYLE		F	came from Sooey
MARY	BOYLE		F	m. ? Scanlon
MICHAEL	BOYLE	1858	F	
WINIFRED	BOYLE	1868	F	**
KATE	SCANLON	1883	F	Mother was Mary Scanlon, nee Boyle
THOMAS	SCANLON	1885	F	Mother was Mary Scanlon, nee Boyle
MARGARET A	SCANLON	1890	F	Mother was Mary Scanlon, nee Boyle
WINIFRED	SCANLON	1891	F	Mother was Mary Scanlon, nee Boyle
?	McGOWAN		G	
?	McGOWAN		G	
MICHAEL	McGOWAN	1849	G	
JOHN	McGOWAN	1851	G	Ballyconnell/Cloonagh
MARTIN	McGOWAN	1860	G	
PETER	MEEHAN	1884	G	Yeats Tavern Connection
MARY JANE	McGOWAN	1889	G	
DORA	McGOWAN	1891	G	
?	BRADY		H	
PATRICK	BRADY		H	
JOHN	BRADY	1885	H	
HENRY	BRADY	1889	H	
ELLEN (HELENA)	BRADY	1895	H	
ANNA	BRADY	1897	H	**
ANNIE B	BRADY	1912	H	l.

Christian Name	Surname	Born	House	Notes	
MARY ELLEN	BRADY	1912	H	l.	
MAGGIE	BRADY	1914	H		
SARAH	BRADY	1916	H		
PATRICK	BRADY	1917	H	m. Mary Jane Brady of Ho. J z.	
HENRY	BRADY	1919	H		
PADDY JOE	BRADY	1932	H	z.	
?	BRADY		I		
SEAN	BRADY		I		
CATHERINE	BRADY	1815	I		
HENRY	BRADY	1856	I		
PATRICK	BRADY	1858	I		
JOHN	BRADY	1859	I		
BRIDGET	BRADY	1865	I	**	
PATRICK	BRADY	1865	I	**	
MARY ANN	BRADY	1869	I	**	
MARGARET	BRADY	1871	I	**	z.
BRIDGET	BRADY	1873	I	**	
NORA	BRADY	1875	I	**	
BRIDGET	BRADY	1879	I	**	
MICHAEL	BRADY	1888	I	m. Ellie Harte of Cloonagh	z.
MARIA	BRADY	1890	I		
BRIDGET	BRADY	1893	I		
ELLEN BEE	BRADY	1895	I		
JANE	BRADY	1897	I		
PATRICK	BRADY	1899	I		
DAN	BRADY	1901	I		
NORA	BRADY	1907	I		
JOHN	BRADY	1928	I	l. Maugherow	z.
DAN	BRADY	1929	I	l. Maugherow	z.
BERNARD	BRADY	1930	I	l. U.S.A.	z.
MARY	BRADY	1931	I	l. U.S.A.	z.
TERESA	BRADY	1932	I	l. Ballyconnell; Mrs Currid	z.
ETNA	BRADY	1933	I	l. U.S.A., a nun	z.
MICHAEL STEPHEN	BRADY	1935	I	l. Luton	z.
BRIDGET	BRADY	1937	I	?l. England	z.
EVELYN	BRADY	1937	I		z.
JANE	BRADY	1938	I	l. Sligo, w. St. John's	z.
ANN	BRADY	1939	I		z.
PATRICK	BRADY	1940	I	l. Ballyconnell	z.
PAID	BRADY		J	son of original Sean, e. 19th c.	
BRIDGET	BRADY	1868	J	**	
MICHAEL	BRADY	1868	J		
HENRY	BRADY	1881	J		
MICHAEL	BRADY	1887	J		
PAT	BRADY	1908	J		

Christian Name	Surname	Born	House	Notes	
MICHAEL	BRADY	1910	J		
MARTIN	BRADY	1911	J		
AGNES	BRADY	1912	J	l. Sligo: Mrs Egan	
KATHLEEN	BRADY	1915	J	m. John Francis Heraughty	
MARY JANE	BRADY	1916	J	l. Moneygold; m. Patrick Brady	z.
JOHN	BRADY	1920	J	l.	z.
OWEN	BRADY	1920	J	l. England	z.
THOMAS	BRADY	1925	J		z.
?	DONLON		K		
? son	DONLON		K	d. in 1920s, aged about 5 years	
KATHLEEN	HOEY		K	m. James Donlon, Agharow	
MICHAEL	HOEY	1851	K		
BRIAN	HOEY	1856	K		
MARY ANN	DONLON	1881	K	m. James D from Lough Rd. Cloonagh	
BRIDGET	DONLON	1888	K		
JOHN	DONLON	1889	K		
THOMAS J.	DONLON	1891	K	**	
MARY ANN	DONLON	1892	K		
ELLEN (HELINA)	DONLON	1893	K		
JAMES	DONLON	1896	K		
KATE	DONLON	1900	K		
JOSEPH	DONLON	1902	K	m. Mary Ann Heraughty of Ho L	z.
ANNIE BRIDGET	DONLON	1924	K	z.	
JOHN	DONLON	1928	K	z.	
NORA	DONLON	1928	K	l. Collooney; Mrs Ewing	z.
PATRICK	DONLON	1931	K	l.	z.
JAMES	DONLON	1936	K	l. England	z.
MARY CATHERINE	DONLON	1938	K	l. England	z.
MARGARET	DONLON	1939	K	l. Australia	z.
?	HERAUGHTY		L		
?	HERAUGHTY		L		
?	HERAUGHTY		L		
?	HERAUGHTY		L		
?	HERAUGHTY		L		
?	HERAUGHTY		L		
?	HERAUGHTY		L		
MICHAEL	HERAUGHTY	1859	L		
MICHAEL	HERAUGHTY	1870	L		
PATRICK	HERAUGHTY	1873	L		
NORA	HERAUGHTY	1874	L	**	
JOAN	HERAUGHTY	1876	L	**	
DAN	HERAUGHTY	1879	L		z.
JACK	HERAUGHTY	1882	L		
ELLEN BRIDGET	HERAUGHTY	1895	L		
MARY ANN	HERAUGHTY	1906	L	m. Joseph Donlon of Ho K	z.
ELLEN BRIDGET	HERAUGHTY	1909	L		

Christian Name	Surname	Born	House	Notes
AGNES	HERAUGHTY	1912	L	
TERESA	HERAUGHTY	1914	L	
JANE	HERAUGHTY	1917	L	l. Moneygold; m. Dominick Harte z.
MARGARET ANN	HERAUGHTY	1922	L	l. Monegold; Mrs. Gillespie z.
ELLEN	MANNION		M	
MARTIN	MANNION	1853	M	
PATRICK	MANNION	1857	M	
JOHN	MANNION	1865	M	
ANDREW	MANNION	1871	M	
JOHN	MANNION	1872	M	
JAMES	MANNION	1879	M	
MARY ANN	MANNION	1880	M	m. Michael Waters z.
JOSEPH	MANNION	1882	M	
CATHERINE	MANNION	1895	M	
?	DUNLEAVY		O	
?	DUNLEAVY		O	
?	DUNLEAVY		O	
?	DUNLEAVY		O	
?	DUNLEAVY		O	
?	DUNLEAVY		O	
?	DUNLEAVY		O	
?	DUNLEAVY		O	
?	DUNLEAVY		O	
?	DUNLEAVY		O	
? daughter	DUNLEAVY		O	m. Padraig McGowan, Cloonagh
THOMAS	DUNLEAVY	1866	O	
MARY	DUNLEAVY	1875	O	**
ANN	DUNLEAVY	1877	O	**
JOHN	DUNLEAVY	1879	O	**
MARY ANN	DUNLEAVY	1881	O	**
JAMES	DUNLEAVY	1883	O	**

The following three were non-natives who married in and were part of the final group of 46 who left Inishmurray in 1948.

ELLIE	BRADY		I	nee Harte of Cloonagh z.
MARY A.	BRADY		J	nee McCann of Ballyconnell z.
MARY	HERAUGHTY		L	nee McCormack of Ballyconnell z.

The following codes apply in the notes column: d. = dead (for recent deaths only); l. = living (and stating where if known); m. = married; w. = working (stating where); z. = one of the final group of 46 who left the island of Inishmurray in 1948; ** = recorded in Ahamlish Register; otherwise from roll book or personal knowledge

Of the 257 births of those born to people living on Inishmurray, we have the year of birth plus or minus one, for all but 68 of them and these span the century from 1841 to 1940; the year given for Catherine Brady, born 1815, may well be a transcription error as the next recorded year of birth is 1841. The year of birth is derived from the National School roll books, the Ahamlish Parish birth register and personal knowledge. There were births in all but twenty-two of the years of the century from 1841 to 1940. Half of these birthless years were in the two decades of the famine. The period from 1868 to 1895 saw the greatest numbers of children being born. The years 1868, 1879 and 1912, with six births each, and 1871, 1882, 1890 and 1895, with five each, had the highest birth rates.

There are 110 males and 115 females on the list; we do not know the sex of the remaining thirty-two. There was only one set of twins born, Dan and Martin being twin boys to John and Mary Heraughty born in 1890. They both died of pulmonary tuberculosis at the age of 34, one on Inishmurray and the other in New York. The commonest of the fifteen male christian names used were John, Michael and Patrick. The commonest of the twenty-one female christian names used were Mary, Bridget and Kate. We have no record of the Christian names of fifty people.

There are other family surnames associated with the island besides those in Appendix 3. The tomb of Maoilen O'Dálaigh, who died on All Souls Day 1612, is beside the *Clocha Breaca*. Currid, O'Leary and Meehan were on the island at the time of the 1802 resettlement. Beranger records that in 1779 there were seven families, regrettably he does not name them, on the island and that several of the girls were seeking boys. When Domhnall Heraughty settled on Inishmurray in 1802 three of the pre-resettlement families, Currid, O'Leary and Meehan, remained on the island for a few years. These were probably families who had no male successors or from which such successors had left the island. It may be no more than pure coincidence that, as mentioned elsewhere, the Meehans of Ballaghameehan were the coarbs of Molaise. Daniel Meehan, who once owned what is now the Yeats Tavern on the north side of Drumcliffe Bridge, claimed to be a descendant or relative of Meehans from Inishmurray. The O'Leary and Meehan families lived under one roof, houses D and E, to the east side of the lane leading to the cashel. The Currid house was the second last, house L, before the school; later this was the house of Dan Heraughty Mick. Houses D and E are the only surviving pre-1802 houses; the present house L is built on site of original Currid house.

O'Rourke records that "Only a few of older people spoke English" at the end of the last century. In my youth there were eight native speakers but only one, Domnick "Crimley" Harte (C) at the evacuation. The others were Mary Heraughty, nee Donlon from Maugherow (D), John and Ann Boyle and Mary Scanlon, nee Boyle, (All F), Michael McGowan and Bridget Donlon, nee McGowan, (both G) and Michael Hoey (K).

CHAPTER 1 – Ancient Monastic Island

1. The larger pool was formed by damming the main drain on the island. This was done in 1950 by some people who tried to run sheep on the island after the islanders had left.

CHAPTER 2 – Prehistoric Site and Monastic Remains

1. *The Annals of Ireland* (Four Masters) gave the date as 555 A.D., while *The Annals of Ulster* place it as 561 A.D.

2. The Queen's writ, which would have brought with it the Reformation, did not run in north Sligo until the early seventeenth century.

3. *The Early Development of Irish Society* by E.R. Norman and J.K.S. St. Joseph asserts, in a statement apparently traced to Westropp, that "the remaining buildings ... [were] kept in reasonable order by the islanders, who used them for storage and cattle until their own quite recent desertion of the island". This is incorrect: the buildings were not used for storage or by cattle. The remains of a turnstile gate can still be seen near the entrance to the cashel. This had been the gate to the cashel for the twenty-three years before the islanders left Inishmurray and replaced an earlier swing gate that had rusted and allowed a donkey to wander into the cashel and break some of the wreaths on a grave there. One may ask why the islanders would house cattle in roofless buildings, or what kind of storage they could be used for, when each household had adequate well-roofed byres and barns.

4. Compare this version from the *Martyrology of Donegal* in which it is said that they met at the cross of *Ath Imlaise* – Ahamlish, on the mainland.

5. The error may have arisen from nasalising the final "n" of *riain* to "r" giving *riair* instead of *riain*. The *riair* was then expanded by O'Donovan to *righ*, fear, and translated "Kingly (*Righ*-King) men".

6. T.H. Mason's *Islands of Ireland* provides an account of the experiences of one such mainland group who were storm-bound on the island after performing the traditional station.

7. As there are no surrounding walls at the last five stations inside the cashel, only one circuit was made at each station.

8. While *hic dormit* does occur on one of the Clonmacnoise stones, Professor Macalister argues on the basis of the lettering that it is a late addition.

9. Wakeman's *A Survey of the Antiquarian Remains of the Island of Innishmurray* was published in 1893.

CHAPTER 3 – Archaeological Material from the Monastic Settlement

1. This is the same Beranger who recorded that a cart-load of oysters could be bought at Aughris for one shilling (5p). One shilling was a respectable sum in 1779, but even then a cart-load was a lot of oysters.

2. It is unclear whether Tadhg O'Heraughty was a tenant of Gore-Booth or Hipsley and Sullivan.

3. Note the clever use of the English form "Jack" in the patronymic to avoid a clumsy "*Sheáin Sheáin*", the pronounciation of which would be "Yawin Yawin".

CHAPTER 4 – Settlement and Re-settlement

1. The name Duthie is to this day associated with the fishing industry in Scotland.

2. That people on a small island should have horses may, now, seem strange but one must recollect that the donkey was not introduced to Ireland until after the Peninsular War (1812). Its usefulness had been noted in Spain.

3. Real *duileasc* is a large coarse variety of seaweed that grows on sea rods.

4. The name "barm" for baker's yeast is retained in a line from an island satirical ballad "for out of the barm the poteen is ran". The word poteen would not have been used except satirically.

5. *Fulachta fiadha* were ancient Irish outdoor cooking places. A trough was dug in the ground and filled with water while a fire was lit nearby with stones heating in it. When the stones were fully heated, they were thrown

into the trough, bringing the water to boiling-point. The meat, wrapped in straw, was then placed in the water to cook, while the temperature was kept at simmering-point by the addition of further hot stones.

CHAPTER 6 – Social Life and Customs

1.   English in the first line later became "Free State".

CHAPTER 7 – Learning and Law

1.   John O'Donovan was on the island in 1836 and does not mention the R.I.C. barracks. Moreover, in 1836 Pádraig O'Heraughty was still alive and it was not until Pádraig had died and his widow re-married that his house, which became the R.I.C. barracks, was vacant.

ILLUSTRATIONS

We thank the following organisations and individuals who supplied illustrations:
The Admiralty, London 42; Authors Collection 50 bottom, 56, 60 top right and bottom, 66, 70; British Museum 36; Champion Art Studios, 26 top; Jim Eccles 16; George Gmelch 21,23, 28, 30, 34, 64, 70, 72 top and bottom, 74; Professor Michael Herity 12, 18, bottom 24; James Hughes 54; National Museum of Ireland 33, 39; Office of Public Works 35 bottom left and right; Ordnance Survey, Dublin 10-11, 76; Adrian Slattery 14; Wakeman, W.F., *A Survey of the Antiquarian Remains on the Island of Inishmurray* being the extra volume of the Royal Society of Antiquaries of Ireland for 1892, London: Williams and Norgate, 1893, 24 top, 34 top left, 41 top right and left, Wakeman Collection Sligo Public Library 3, 6, 24 top; Welsh Collection, Ulster Museum 26 bottom, 28, 46, 63.

BIBLIOGRAPHY

Annals

(All in Royal Irish Academy)
Annals of Loch Cé
Annals of Tigernach
Chronicum Scotorum
Cogadh Gaedheal re Gallaibh
Felire of Oengus
Martyrology of Donegal
Martyrology of Gorman
Silva Gadelica

Books and Articles

Bailey, Richard N., "An Early Irish Carved Stone in Northern England", *Journal of the Royal Society of Antiquaries of Ireland,* Vol. 120 (1990), 126-128.
Bergh, Stefan, *Landscape of the Monuments, A Study of the Passage Tombs in the Cuil Irra Region, Co. Sligo, Ireland,* Stockholm, 1995.
Bernelle, Agnes, ed., *Decantations: A Tribute to Maurice Craig,* Dublin 1992.
Bourke, Cormac, "Early Irish Hand Bells", *Journal of the Royal Society of Antiquaries of Ireland,* Vol. 110 (1980), 52-66.
Bourke, Cormac, "A Crozier and Bell from Inishmurray and their place in Ninth-Century Irish Archaeology", *Proceedings of the Royal Irish Academy,* Vol. 85 C5 (1985), 145-168 & Pl. I-VII.

Collingwood-Bruce, J., *A Descriptive Catalogue of Antiquities, Chiefly British, at Alnwick Castle*, Newcastle-upon-Tyne, 1880.

Cotton, Don C.F., *The Heritage of Inishmurray*, Sligo 1989.

Crawford, Allan, *Tristan da Cunha and the Roaring Forties*, London 1982.

Ferguson Samuel, "The Burial of King Cormac Mac Airt" in *The Poems of Samuel Ferguson*, edited by Padraic Colum. Dublin: Figgis, 1963.

Gregory, Lady, *Visions and Beliefs in the West of Ireland.*

Grose, Francis, *The Antiquities of Ireland*, Vol. II, 1795.

Harbison, Peter, *Pilgrimage in Ireland, The Monuments and the People*, Barrie and Jenkins, London 1991.

Henry, Rev. William, *Hints Towards a Natural Typographical History of the Counties Sligo, Donegal, Fermanagh and Lough Erne,* 1739. National Archives Manuscript 2533.

Heraughty, Paddy, "Inishmurray – Sligo's Sacred Isle", *Ireland of the Welcomes,* Vol. 42, No. 5, Sept.Oct. 1993, 27-33.

Herity, Michael, "The Buildings and Layout of Early Irish Monasteries before the Year 1000", Montreal: Monastic Studies 1983.

Ireland, Aideen, "Roger Chambers Walker" in Timoney, forthcoming.

Mahr, Adolph, and Joseph Raftery, *Christian Art in Ancient Ireland,* 1932 & 1941, reprint New York 1976.

Mason, T.H., *Islands of Ireland,* 1936; Cork, Mercier Press 1967.

Meehan, Rev. Denis, *Molaise of Inishmurray*, 1989.

MacCarthaigh, Mícheál, "Placenames of Inishmurray", *Dinnseanchas* 4 (1971): 60-72

McParlan, James, *Statistical Survey of the County Sligo*, Dublin: Graisberry and Campbell, 1802.

McTernan, John, *Memory Harbour, The Port of Sligo*, Sligo 1992.

O'Farrell, Fergus, "The Inishmurray Statue of St. Molaise: a Re-assessment", *Figures from the Past: Studies on Figurative Art in Christian Ireland in honour of Helen M. Roe,* Ed. Etienne Rynne, Dublin 1987, 205-208.

O'Crohan, Thomas, *The Islandman*, Dublin: Talbot Press, 1934.

O'Donovan, John, ed., *Annals of the Kingdom of Ireland by the Four Masters,* Dublin: Irish Archaeological and Celtic Society, 1851.

O'Donovan, John, "Sligo Letters", *Ordnance Survey Letters*, No. 36 (8 July 1836). Dublin: Royal Irish Academy.

O'Rourke, Terence, *History of Sligo: Town and County*, Dublin: James Duffy 1889.

Petty, Sir William, *History of the Cromwellian Survey of Ireland, A.D. 1655-6 (The Down Survey)*, edited by T.A. Larcom, Dublin: Irish Archaeological and Celtic Society, 1851.

Protesant Penny Magazine, The, No. 5, 25 October 1834, Vol. I. and continued in No. 7, 1 January 1835. Not referred to in the text, the article is in the main a diatribe against the Roman Catholic religion, couched in the most intemperate language and adds nothing to our knowledge of the island. The one reference to the cross-inscribed pillar stones is a variance with recorded fact. The article is not signed but in a recent catalogue is given as "edited by the notorious apostle of Achill".

Rynne, Etienne, *"Dun Aengus and Some Similar Celtic Ceremonial Centres",* Bernelle 1992, 196-207

Stokes, William, *The Life and Labours in Art and Archaeology of George Petrie*, LI.D., M.R.I.A., London 1868.

Timoney, Martin A., ed., Sligo Field Club Commemorative Volume, forthcoming.

Vallency, Charles, *A Vindication of the Ancient History of Ireland*, Dublin 1786.

Wakeman, W.F., "Inish Muiredaich, now Inishmurray, and its antiquities", *Journal of the Royal Society of Antiquaries of Ireland,* Vol. 17 (1885), 175-332.

Wakeman, W.F., *A Survey of the Antiquarian Remains on the Island of Inishmurray* being the extra volume of the Royal Society of Antiquaries of Ireland for 1892, London: Williams and Norgate, 1893.

Wakeman, W.F., VI – "The Oaken Statue of St. Molaise, on Inishmurray, Co. Sligo", *Graves and Monuments of Illustrious Irishmen*, pp. 12-14.

Walker, Roger Chambers, *Account Book of Roger Chambers Walker of Rathcarrick, 1836 to 1845,* Manuscript, Sligo Library.

Wilde, William, "Memoir of Gabriel Beranger, and his labours in the cause of Irish art, literature, and antiquities from 1760 to 1780, with illustrations", *Journal of the Royal Society of Antiquaries of Ireland*, 11 (1870-71), 33-64,

121-152.

Wilde, William: *Memoir of Gabriel Beranger, and his labours in the cause of Irish Art and Antiquities, from 1760 to 1780,* Dublin 1880.

Wood-Martin, W. G., *History of Sligo*, Vol. I, 1882.

News Reports

"The State of Innishmurray." *Sligo Independent*, 24 February 1883.

"Innishmurray Island Again." *Sligo Independent*, 3 March 1883.

"Relief to Innishmurray." *Sligo Independent,* 19 May 1883.

"Sligo Board of Guardians." *Sligo Independent*, 19 May 1883.

Sligo Independent, 23 June 1883.

"Sligo Board of Guardians." *Sligo Independent*, 19 January 1895.

"Innishmurray Island to be Evacuated." *Sligo Independent,* 24 December 1897.

"A Strange Phenomena." *Sligo Independent*, 6 March 1906.

"Obituary of Domnick Harte." (Crimley) *Sligo Independent*, 11 June 1949.

"Late King of Innishmurray Island, Sligo." *Sligo Independent* 17 February 1951.